THE COMPLETE AND UTTER WALLY

THE COMPLETE AND UTTER WALLY

comprising *How To Be A Wally* and *Superwally*

PAUL MANNING

A Moon and Parrot Publication
from
Macdonald

A Macdonald Book

Part I first published by Futura Publications in 1983
as HOW TO BE A WALLY

Part II first published by Futura Publications in 1984
as SUPERWALLY

This edition published in Great Britain in 1985 by Macdonald
& Co (Publishers) Ltd, London & Sydney

British Library Cataloguing in Publication Data

Manning, Paul
Complete and utter wally.
I. Title
828′.91409 PR6063.A38/

ISBN 0–356–12140–2

Printed and bound in Great Britain by
Redwood Burn Limited, Trowbridge, Wiltshire
Bound at The Dorstel Press

Macdonald & Co (Publishers) Ltd
Maxwell House
74 Worship Street
London EC2A 2EN

A BPCC plc Company

CONTENTS

PART I — HOW TO BE A WALLY

PART II — SUPERWALLY

HOW TO BE A WALLY

INTRODUCTION

Every year, at a glittering ceremony televised live from the heart of London's West End, a distinguished group of men and women from all walks of life step forward to receive what are now widely regarded as Britain's highest, most prestigious and most coveted public honours: the celebrated 'Wally of the Year' Awards.

The sheer range of different categories is enormous: from Radio One Wally of the Year (current joint title-holders: lovebirds Janice Long and Peter Powell) to Sports Wally of the Year (current title-holder: 'Sulky' Steve Davis); from Wally Coffee-Table Theologian of the Year (the Bishop of Durham) to Wearer of the Most Hideous Knitwear on a TV Panel Game (David Coleman) – and so to such hotly contested titles as Right Royal Superwally of the Year, Performer of the Year's Most Fatuous Pop single, and of course, finally All-Round Showbiz Wally of the Year – an honour currently held by Terry Wogan, who swept to an easy victory in the 1985 awards by falling flat on his face on the opening night of his new three-times-weekly chat show.

Of all the awards in recent times, however, few have aroused such intense public interest as those for outstanding achievement in the political field. Past winners here have included International Superwally Ronald Reagan, for his sensitive handling of the V.E. Day commemorations; John Selwyn Gummer, for revealing that he has the words SEX SEX SEX and YES YES YES emblazoned on his pillows; Defence Secretary Michael Heseltine, voted Gung-Ho Tory Wally of the Year for his gallantry in booting out a handful of Quakers, peace-protesters and other riff-raff from the Molesworth Cruise Missile Base while dressed in a flak jacket two sizes too big for him and assisted by a mere four hundred or so heavily-armed members of the Royal Air Force Police; and last but by no means least, the Scottish contingent of the Federation of Conservative Students, who early in 1985 scored a runaway success in an entirely new category: that of Most Rowdy and Boorish Behaviour by a Bunch of Drunken Hooray Wallies at a Right-wing Party Political Knees-up.

Not surprisingly at a time when TV producers and programme-planners are desperate for any old rubbish to fill up the airwaves, many top Wally award-winners these days are busily carving dazzling careers for themselves in the media: answering phone-ins on *Saturday Superstore* ... hosting *Family Fortunes* ... having their fortune told by Russell Grant ... getting insulted by Russell Harty ... making embarrassing guest appearances on Michael Parkinson's *All Star Secrets* ... Often, of course, that's how they win their Wally awards in the first place.

But success as a Wally isn't something to be measured just in terms of fame, public adulation and top TV ratings. There are thousands of complete Wallies all over the country who work hard and never achieve recognition. Many happily spend half their lives squirting Orange Fanta down their front, chucking litterbins around pub car-parks and stuffing paper towels down British Rail toilets, and precisely because they *are* Wallies, they expect no greater reward for all their efforts than a sopping wet T-shirt, a £25 fine, and a ten-minute bollocking from an irate Inter-City guard fresh out of Customer Care school.

So what *is* a Wally? And how do you become one?

This book holds the answers. but first, a few definitions.

What is a Wally?

A Wally, in case you didn't know, is someone who keeps the current issue of the *TV Times* in an embossed imitation leather binder. He drives a customised Cortina with NOLANS in white letters on his windscreen visor, Go Faster stripes down the sides and a sticker on the rear window that reads 'My Other Car's a Porsche'. At rock concerts, Wallies are easy to spot: they're the ones who climb on each others' shoulders and wave their arms around in time to the music or bob up and bown at the back playing imaginary guitars.

Many Wallies are also headbangers, but it doesn't necessarily follow. All headbangers, however, are by definition Wallies.

A Wally is someone who has a sticker on his steering wheel saying 'Belt Up – Be a Life-saver', and still forgets to wear a seatbelt. He buys a roll of nylon lawn to lay in his garden, tries to cut it with a Flymo and accidentally slices through the flex. Sometimes he shaves his chest hair to try and stimulate the growth.

The person who sabotaged your office vending machine by sticking foreign coins in it was probably a Wally. Those people you see waving fluffy toys and scarves and grinning inanely at you from the back of coaches are definitely Wallies. The fast-talking prat in the Harry Fenton suit who tries to sell you double-glazing and tells you he's installed it in his home is a Wally. If you believe him, you're a bigger Wally than he is, and you won't be needing this book after all.

The couple walking down the street in front of you arm in arm with their hands resting lightly on each others' bottoms are Wallies. Your boss became a Wally when he dressed up as Santa Claus at the office Christmas Party and handed out worthless trinkets to all the office Wallettes. *Things* can be Wally too. Blob lamps are Wally. Artificial snow is Wally. Leatherette is Wally. The tinsel hanging at the back of car showrooms is Wally.

Being a Wally is a doddle – a piece of cake. Right?

Wrong. Being a Wally is not just a question of splashing yourself with Brut, swanning around in an acrylic sweater, or taking the occasional joy-ride in a supermarket trolley. It *is* all these things, but it's also a great deal more. It can mean standing outside D.E.R. showrooms in the pouring rain watching *Game For A Laugh.* Or boldly stepping out of your car in Windsor Safari Park to offer prawn-cocktail flavoured crisps to the lions. Or braving carbon monoxide poisoning by picnicking within inches of passing juggernauts. Or riding three at a time on coin-operated rocking horses in C & A. Often it means risking life and limb. In some cases your own.

Above all, being a Wally is a state of mind. It's writing glowing testimonials in the visitors' book of a Little Chef – and meaning every word of it. It's not being able to work out the right-of-way system at a mini-roundabout. It's preferring Coffeemate to milk. It's being genuinely unable to tell the difference between Stork and butter, and proud of it.

Can anybody be a Wally?

Sadly, one thing this book will teach you is that not everybody can be a Wally, let alone a Superwally. Let's be brutally realistic about this. Some people are destined to remain boring old total non-Wallies all their lives and there's nothing anybody can do to help them. Maybe they were deprived of the right kind of stimulus in early childhood – the Yorkie bars, the chance to browse through Mum's Julio Iglesias albums, watch Roland Rat and the gang on Breakfast TV, or flip through Dad's week-by-week pictorial encyclopedia of the world's great elite breeds of fighting men. Maybe when other kids were out posting Kentucky Fried chicken boxes through old ladies' letterboxes, they preferred to stay at home glued to the Open University. Maybe their parents were never prepared to make the sacrifices or give them the breaks. Who knows? Maybe they never had it in them from the start.

That's the bad news.

The *good* news is that Wallies are definitely on the increase. Look around you. You can probably think of at least one dedicated full-timer in your own immediate circle of acquaintance. Time was when there was one in every office. Now a whole gang of Office Wallies come roaring back from the Moon and Parrot every lunchtime and spend the entire afternoon pinching bottoms, chucking darts at Playboy centrefolds and flicking rubber bands at each other.

There are other pointers to this massive upsurge in the Wally population. In the past you could often see the odd pair or handful of Wallies gamely knocking back the duty-free booze and lurching drunkenly around the passenger lounges on cross-Channel ferries. Nowadays they're coming out of the portholes. In fact, so many Wallies seem willing to part with hard cash for a chance to throw up in the English Channel that the more far-sighted ferry operators are even laying on special day-trips for this very purpose.

Perhaps most significant of all, there are encouraging signs that other countries are beginning to wake up to the Wally lifestyle. Without wishing to sound chauvinistic, this is almost certainly due to the selfless missionary zeal of hordes of British Wallies who've flocked to tourists traps all over Europe just to show the locals how it's done – often risking harsh treatment from armies of uniformed killjoys and jackbooted petty bureaucrats. Many British Wallies have even had to suffer fines and imprisonment at the hands of narrow-minded Continental officialdom – usually for so-called 'crimes' no more serious than the wrecking of nightclubs and discos, the wholesale looting of shops and the deliberate burning down of hotels. Fortunately this doesn't seem to have put them off in the slightest. Quite the opposite: it's simply made them all the more determined to go back and have another bash next year.

The Complete Wally Promise

The Complete and Utter Wally is a fully comprehensive guide covering every aspect of the subject, from first steps in Wallydom through to Superwallydom and beyond.

And to show that the author and the publishers of this book have complete confidence in its effectiveness in every case, we are prepared to offer a unique and unprecedented guarantee.

If any reader, having bought a copy of *The Complete and Utter Wally* and read it thoroughly from beginning to end, genuinely believes that he has not become a Complete Wally as a result, then he has the right to return the book to wherever he bought it and say, 'I have bought this copy of *The Complete and Utter Wally* and I can honestly say I'm as sick as a parrot because frankly it just hasn't worked for me.'

The bookseller will then fall about laughing and when he recovers, grasp him by the hand and say: 'Congratulations, son – you've made it at last!'

GET IT RIGHT

How to achieve Wally credibility

In order to be a true Wally you must have Wally credibility. This means not only being a Wally, but showing the scars to prove it.

There are various immediately recognisable signs of Wally credibility. A leg or arm in plaster, for instance, gives Wally credibility – particularly if the plaster has been signed by all your Wally friends. An inverted coat hanger in place of an aerial on your car can give Wally credibility, and so can fibreglass patches on the bodywork, suggesting hours of toil in the garage. Any wounds or injuries received in the course of DIY projects give Wally credibility: fingers missing; lacerations caused by careless use of a Black and Decker sanding disc. The same applies to love bites and tattoos.

If you have the right kind of Wally credibility – the kind that comes from knocks and bruises sustained in the hard school of life – you'll be confident and secure enough not to feel you have to make a great song and dance about these things. They'll be part of you. You'll be content to let people notice them and draw their own conclusions. When a friend reminds you admiringly how one New Year's Eve you scaled Nelson's Column and sprayed 'Hissing Sid is innocent' all over it with an aerosol, you'll simply shrug modestly and say, 'It was nothing ... ' This won't be false modesty on your part: just an honest recognition that what you did was neither more nor less than your *duty* as a Wally.

Certain possessions can act as Wally credibility boosters: a darts trophy on the mantelpiece; a plastic motorway cone or stolen lifebelt on top of the wardrobe; a beer tankard with the owner's name engraved on it hanging behind the bar at the Moon and Parrot. All these things discreetly declare to friends and acquaintances that whoever owns them is a Wally.

Naturally, as a beginner, you want to know how to get

hold of these vital pieces of equipment without going through the gruelling apprenticeship your more accomplished fellow-Wallies have already survived.

Unfortunately, it can't be done. There *are* no short cuts. Wally credibility has to be earned. The most that you can hope for is to avoid needlessly blowing your credibility by some elementary blunder. And that's where this section *can* help.

Here then are a few tips to start off with:

1) In order not to blow your Wally credibility you must remember that sports kit must be spotlessly laundered and overalls must be covered with filthy and unmentionable stains – *never* the other way round.

2) Your score on the Space Invaders should either be astronomically high (suggesting that you practise every minute of the day) or pitifully low (suggesting that you will never be any good at it no matter how much you practise) – *never* merely middling or respectable.

3) If you are unfortunate enough to possess a clean driving licence, *never* produce it in the company of your fellow-Wallies.

4) *On no account* leave Penguin Classics on the rear window ledge of your car (or as you should learn to call it, 'motor') alongside the nodding dogs and fluffy dice. This could damage your Wally credibility so seriously that you might never regain your friends' esteem – not even by showing that you can remember the words of an entire Bucks Fizz number and can perform the dance steps too.

Wally Etiquette

Another way to blow your Wally credibility is to commit some unwitting breach of Wally Etiquette. Wally Etiquette consists of the following crucial points:

1) When travelling on the tube, you will entertain other passengers by swinging from the straps like a monkey, chasing other Wallies up and down the carriage, and needlessly obstructing the doors with your foot.
2) When entering a building via swing doors, always go round at least twice and before exiting, give them a hefty push so that anyone still left inside gets their arms and legs crushed.
3) When travelling on a main-line train, it is essential to sit in the luggage rack, scratch your initials on the mirrors, and when leaving, open the door and spring out before the train has stopped moving.
4) On noticing a television interview being conducted outside a football ground or in a shopping centre, be sure either to loiter inanely in the middle distance or to crowd around with a group of other Wallies, pulling funny faces, shouting 'Hello, Mum' and giving thumbs-up signs to the camera.
5) In restaurants, always address the waiter as 'John' and show your appreciation of a really first-class Chicken Vindaloo by swilling it down with at least three pints of Black Label and regurgitating the lot on the pavement outside.
6) Do not smoke between courses. Try and keep a fag on the go throughout the meal.
7) When forced to tell a bare-faced lie, always preface it with the words, 'I'll be honest with you'.
8) On finishing a packet of crisps in a pub, do not forget to blow it up and burst it, showering people with the leftover bits at the bottom of the bag and causing them to spill their drinks.
9) After giving vent to a stream of four-letter words, always ask your listeners to pardon your French.

1 'I'm all there for a pint of Black Label'
2A 'Wauurrrrrr!!' or alternatively....
2B ....'Woooaaaargh!!' (Instant Pavlovian response to words 'Bo Derek')

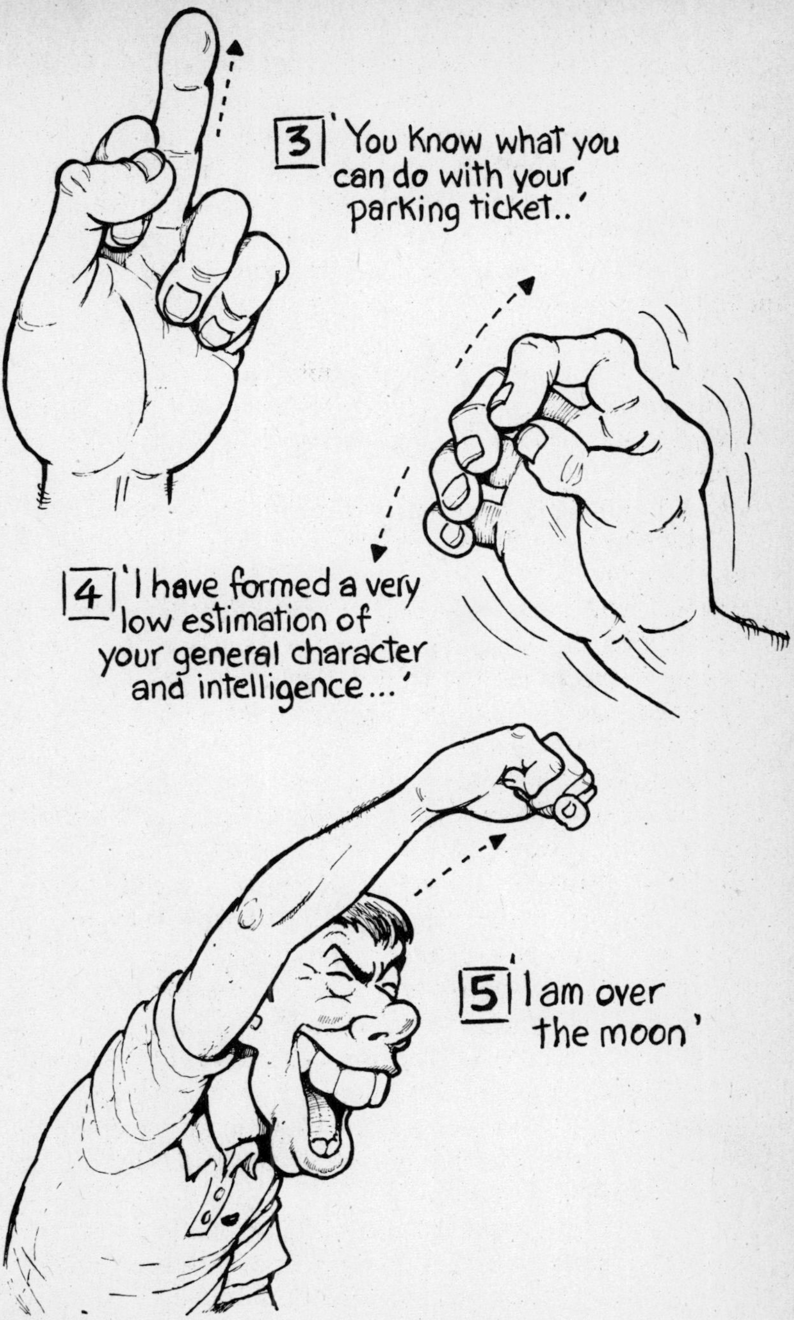
3 'You know what you can do with your parking ticket..'
4 'I have formed a very low estimation of your general character and intelligence...'
5 'I am over the moon'

How to talk like a Wally

There's no quicker or easier way to lose what little Wally credibility you have in these crucial early stages than to let slip the wrong word or phrase. How many would-be-Wally shop assistants, for instance, have seen all their hopes dashed simply because they greeted customers with the words 'Can I help you?' instead of the more correct, 'What can I do you for?' To avoid Batemanesque scenes, observe the following rules:

1) On colliding with a police patrol car while practising your emergency stops in a busy suburban high street, express surprise by saying 'Strike a light'. *Not* 'Good heavens'.
2) On winning a huge cash prize in a Reader's Digest Lucky Numbers Draw, you are 'over the moon'. You are *not* 'delighted'.
3) On failing to be selected for the office table football squad, or being given the elbow by your girl-friend and having to go to all the trouble of peeling her name off your windscreen, you are 'sick as a parrot'. You are *not* 'annoyed', 'browned off'.
4) To express agreement with a proposition, *don't* nod or say 'absolutely'. Say, 'this is it'. *E.g*: Wally A: 'You win some, you lose some.' Wally B: 'This is it.'
5) Your Saturday-morning shopping expeditions to Mothercare with the wife are *not* 'a bore'. They are 'a pain in the bum/arse/behind'.
6) The correct response to a joke or amusing remark is 'Like it, like it'. *Not* 'How priceless'.
7) A person who OD's on Ritz Crackers and Sun Pat Blue Cheese Spread is *not* 'a greedy pig', he's a 'gannet'.
8) Your two-week wreck-a-hotel-room-in-all-the-historic-cities-of-Europe coach tour was *not* 'wonderful' or 'marvellous', it was 'magic'.
9) Lastly, in the unlikely event of your finding yourself suddenly thrust into the limelight and asked to make a statement to the news media, do not miss an opportunity to use the words, 'at this moment in time', 'hopefully',

'across the board', 'meaningful dialogue', and to refer at some point to money either 'up front' or 'on the table'.

The following phrases should be banished from your repertoire:

'Within reasonable bounds'

'Off the beaten track'

'A select gathering'

(See also Body Language, pp. 18-19)

Thinking like a Wally

To achieve Wally credibility you must learn to think like a Wally –

– and that means first of all understanding the term *nous*.

Nous is what Wallies have instead of common sense. It's that breezy savoir-faire that enables you to hop without any apparent effort out of one fine mess and straight into another even finer one. It means, for example, knowing short cuts through labyrinthine housing estates that end up by being twice as long as your original route. It also means having at your disposal a vast range of sophisticated labour-saving power-tool attachments in a garage or shack at the bottom of the garden that either fall to pieces or turn out to be lacking some vital component on the one occasion you want to use them. Although nous embraces a number of useful skills – knowing which foreign coins you can use in vending machines or parking meters; how to wind back the clock of your motor; how to bypass gas and electricity meters – it's also to do with *who* you know. It's knowing someone who knows someone else who just might be able to lay his hands on a visor-louvre for the rear window of your Capri – for a price.

Lack of nous can be a handicap for you as an aspiring Wally. In your early shots at DIY, for example, you'll probably muddle along as best you can, putting your foot through walls, burying yourself under piles of plaster dust and masonry and generally being a Bit Of A Wally.

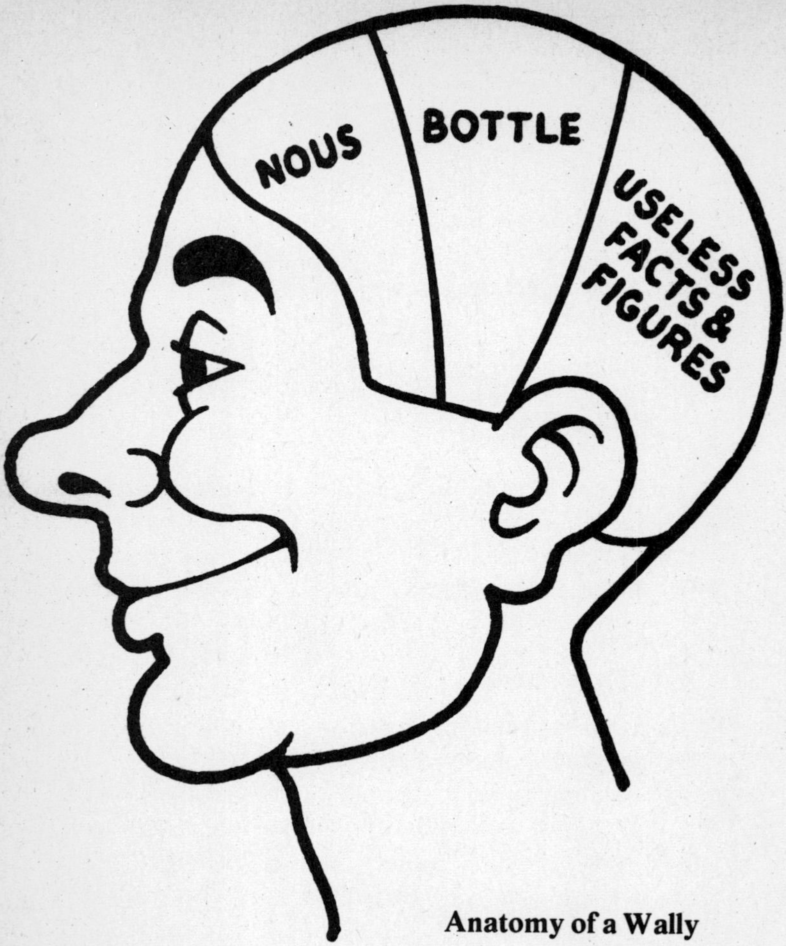

Anatomy of a Wally

If you had a bit more nous, though, you'd have contacts in the trade – cowboys who'd wreak far greater chaos *and* charge you large sums of money for their services. All you'd then have to do is pay them and you'd be right up there among the Complete Wallies.

Unfortunately for you, nous can't be taught in a book. It's something you pick up gradually in the course of being a Wally and mingling with other Wallies. It's made easier

- Nothing beats the great smell of Brut
- Love means never having to say you're sorry
- 99 per cent of all Wallies are caused by accidents
- Every cloud has a sumptuous Wallytex lining
- If you can't stand the heat, get out of the Solarium
- The best things in life are 20p off
- If you can't beat them, try taking up Kung Fu
- Never mind the content,
  admire the hand-tooled binding
- You can't make a silk purse out of a sow's ear
  – but you *can* use it to make a very attractive
  novelty luggage tag.

for you, though, by the fact that they will volunteer, or try to foist, their nous on you whether you're interested or not. When you've acquired it, you can then foist it on other people. You will be able, for instance, to pull in at the roadside when you see a motorist in difficulties, confidently set about taking his engine to bits, still not locate the fault, then find that you can't get the bits back in the right order – at which point you drive off, leaving him considerably worse off than before you arrived.

Bottle is another vital quality for any Wally. It can be defined roughly as: valour minus discretion.

Most Wally activities call for bottle, some more than others. Ordering 'Spling Lolls' in a Chinese Take-Away requires relatively little. Late-night shopping at Key Markets or battling your way up the down escalator during the rush hour require rather more. Striding into a paratroopers' mess and announcing that you thought only fairies had wings requires a great deal.

Whatever activity you're engaged in, the important thing is not to lose your bottle or 'bottle out' halfway through. For instance, when a policeman stops you for speeding the wrong way down a one-way street and asks, 'Didn't you see the arrows?', you should reply promptly, 'Arrows, John? I didn't even see the Indians.' If you simply shrug your shoulders, grin vacantly and mutter something about it being a fair cop, you'll lose valuable Wally credibility points; in fact, you won't be a Wally at all, you'll be a Turkey.

Before concluding this short section on how to think like a Wally, some mention should be made of the contents of your data banks. Do not confuse being a Wally with being an ignoramus. An ignoramus is empty-headed, whereas your head should be sufficiently well-stocked with facts and figures to enable you at least to answer questions on local radio phone-ins and to stand a reasonable chance of winning the latest Duran Duran single or a Return of the Jedi T-shirt – and if possible to score respectably on The Pop Quiz and A Question of Sport as well. Not by actually taking part in the programmes of course, but by shouting out the answers as you watch at home, or even better, as you stand mesmerised in front of banks of television screens in the electrical goods department of Debenham's.

In addition to having an in-depth knowledge of the British Singles Charts and The Guinness Book of Sporting Records, you should also be able to repeat all television lager, Cinzano and Campari commercials verbatim, and your data banks should contain copious scraps of information such as the following:

1) Names of Derby winners since the turn of the century
2) Kevin Keegan's favourite breakfast cereal
3) The combined birthweight of the England 1982 World Cup Squad.
4) Star signs of the famous
5) Barbara Windsor's bust measurement
6) The plots of Every Which Way But Loose, Dirty Harry, Freebie and The Bean, Smokey and The Bandit, Mad Max, Rollerball, Death Race 2000, and Friday The Thirteenth Part Three in 3D
7) The words to *Viva España*
8) Jocky Wilson's preferred brand of underarm deodorant
9) Fiona Richmond's telephone number.

With the help of your data banks, you should also be able to speak authoritatively on the following burning issues:

1) Was God an astronaut?
2) Are the Russians controlling our weather?
3) Prophesies of Nostradamus
4) Dolly Parton: the silicon implant question

The Wally look

Wally credibility means *dressing* like a Wally too.

Many people fondly imagine that all you have to do to achieve the Wally look is to bung on a mouldering T-shirt or acrylic pully in the morning, drag a razor over the bum fluff (slicing the top off a few spots in the process), splash on

The Handsome Brut

The Harlow Harpie

The Acrylic Kid

The Hell's Wally

half a gallon of Brut and thus to go around looking – and in the case of the Hell's Wally, smelling – pretty much like the proverbial pig's breakfast.

Of course, this is a myth.

The Wally Look has to be worked at. Even the dragged-through-a-hedge-backwards look favoured by the Hell's Wally (see p. 27) involves hours of preparation if you're going to Get It Right. It's not just a question of clothes – it's personal grooming too. There's the hair to attend to, the pimples and pustules to anoint with Calomine Lotion; and then comes the purely practical problem of how to insinuate your legs into those festering drainpipe jeans without causing them to disintegrate altogether. The jeans, that is. If you're going to go for the Handsome Brut look (see p. 26), it could take you even longer; sometimes it's months before you find a shampoo that gives your hair that unique Arthur Scargill nylon toupee texture.

Another point that needs to be borne in mind is that the Wally Look is only *partly* to do with the way you dress or the way you comb – or appear not to comb – your hair. Just as important is that indefinable something in the set of your features or your stance generally that marks you out as a Wally – as someone who might well at some point in the past have been bodily ejected from Tiffany's on a Friday night, caught fare-dodging on the Underground, or incarcerated by Spanish police for pouring soap powder into municipal fountains in Madrid during World Cup Final Week. That subtle whiff of the out-and-out Wally can't be faked, just as it can't be taught. You've either Got It or you haven't.

For the time being, though, let's concentrate on what you *can* achieve by selecting the right clothes. The following notes on Wally attire should help you.

Underpants. When it comes to underpants, the true Wally dresses according to a simple maxim: 'If you want to raise a laugh, drop your trousers.' In certain circumstances, the mere act of appearing in public dressed only in your underpants is enough to establish that you're a Wally. But to ram the message home, make sure that your underpants are made of nylon and are inscribed with one or more of these mottos:

- Sex Appeal – Please give generously
- I don't know what ideas *you've* got, lady, but these are staying on.
- Greetings from Loch Ness
- Home of the Jolly Pink Giant
- Prodwell Hydraulic Research Establishment
- Pink and Perky
- Do Not Crush
- Flasher
- Vasectomised

Also acceptable are: American-style boxer shorts, string underpants, bikini briefs, sequinned jockstraps, posing pouches, and any underpants decorated with polka dots, Union Jacks or carnival stripes.

Vests. String vests are quintessentially Wally, and so are T-shirts *worn* as vests. But in both cases they should be clearly visible; either undo the top buttons of your shirt or wear a shirt made out of a man-made fibre that lets the vest or T-shirt show through.

Thermal underwear. This is only Wally if worn during a heatwave.

Trousers. Flared trousers, golfing slacks, Stay-Prest strides or denim jeans with buttons instead of a zip are Wally. All should be worn slightly short in order to display your jazzy socks to full advantage.

Shirts and ties. Matching shirts and ties, Englebert Humperdinck frilly dress shirts, polyester shirts dotted with racing cars, horses or other emblems are all acceptable items of Wally wear. Stripey shirts with white collars are *de rigueur* for the executive Wally (see p. 112), but note that the collars should *not* be detachable. Leisure shirts for disco wear should have giant collars that stretch right across the shoulders.

T-shirts, Sweatshirts, etc. T-shirts form a vital part of the Wally wardrobe, but a T-shirt with the *wrong* design or message on it is a glaring gaffe that can spell social disaster. Unless you're going to proclaim your membership of CAMRA or your loyalty to certain approved rock bands, stick to sanctioned legends such as the following:

- Oh Lord, help me to keep my big mouth shut until I know what I'm talking about
- Too much sex makes you late for work
- I'm with stupid
- Sod Off
- I am a virgin (but this is a very old T-shirt)
- Ormskirk College of Food Technology Rag Week (*or similar*)

Pullovers. Guernsies and hand-knitted originals are *out*! You *might* risk a navy-blue lambswool V-neck with greyhound motif and get away with it in a poor light, but the only way to be really safe is to stick to those Wally classics, the diamond-patterned acrylic eyeball-searer or the heavy-knit white and brown belted cardigan or Wally Warmer.

Shoes. Shoes are the Cinderella of the Wally's wardrobe. Hush Puppies, C & A Trainers, possibly a heavyweight two-tone pair with multicoloured laces for best – it's not wise to sport anything too fancy when a major part of your daily routine consists of kicking Coke cans around shopping precincts, shinning up lamposts and leaping flights of stairs in multi-storey car parks.

Suits. Suits tend to be worn only by executive or business Wallies, or by Wallies attending weddings, funerals or making court appearances following night-club brawls. Should be a three-piece number in black, dark blue or beige enabling the wearer to pass as Vito Corleone's right-hand man.

Personal adornment. No CND or SDP lapel badges, please. Heavy gold signet rings, plastic key-rings in the form of biscuits, gold 'ingot' pendants with the hallmark on the front, identity bracelets, St Christopher medallions, tie clips, arm bracelets, mirror shades, imitation crocodile-skin belts with large buckles in the form of the wearer's initials, belts with purses attached or huge bunches of keys dangling from them: all are acceptable. Many people apparently fail to see the point of wearing an identity bracelet. In fact it has a simple practical purpose. It's for those grim mornings when you wake up with a splitting headache and can't remember who the hell you are.

Recognising your fellow-Wally

Wally credibility means being able to spot another Wally a mile off. The difficulty here is that everybody has their own idea of what a Wally is. You no doubt have yours. The person who cornered you in a train compartment and talked about custom cars all the way from Euston to Inverness was a Wally. The joker in your office who stuck the receiver to your phone with Superglue was a Wally. The bloke down the road who claims to know this bloke who knows this other bloke whose brother's in the S.A.S. is a Wally.

The point is: you think you know. Everybody thinks they know.

In actual fact, spotting a Wally isn't that simple any more.

Not all Wallies go around with woolly bobble hats pulled down over their eyes. There are plainclothes or 'closet' Wallies too: outwardly respectable people doing outwardly respectable jobs who've probably never worn an RAC

Lombard Rally or Avon Tyres anorak in their life; people you'd never suspect of being Wallies – until one day they strip down to their Union Jack underpants and insist on showing you their tattoos.

Then there are the soft-spoken retiring types who wouldn't so much as break wind in a telephone box – until they astonish you at the annual company dinner by leaping to their feet, seizing the nearest microphone, rattling off a stream of side-splitting mother-in-law jokes or celebrity impressions, performing tricks with their toupee and rounding off the act by setting fire to their chest hair with a cigarette lighter.

Even more disconcerting are the people who look like Wallies or are doing jobs traditionally performed by Wallies – sticking labels on tins of Cook-In Sauce at Tescos or selling electrical goods at Comet – who turn out not to be Wallies at all; instead they're History of Art students from Oxford working in their vac, Shirley Conran's offspring slumming it, or journalists gathering data for articles in *New Society*.

So how on earth do you tell? There's no easy answer to this one, but you may find it helpful to consult the guide on pp. 34-35.

The Wally Who's Who

In order to achieve Wally credibility you must know who's who in the Wally World.

So who are the big names? An abridged list of current members of the International Order of the Sick Parrot can be found in the Reference Section at the end of this book, (see p. 122). In the meantime it's also instructive to take a look at a few individuals who for one reason or another *fail* to be Wallies, and ask yourself where they're going wrong.

Why is it, for example, that Paul Gambaccini patently fails to be a Wally, while Peter Powell, Tony Blackburn, Jonathan King and Dave Lee Travis are not only past masters of the art but probably couldn't be anything else if they tried? Is it just to do with his occasional appearances on the arts programme Kaleidoscope, or is there some deeper reason?

Why is it that Sir John Betjeman repeatedly manages to miss being a Wally while his two fellow-wordsmiths Cyril Fletcher and Pam Ayres hit the mark unerringly every time? With all those years of practice behind him, you'd have thought he could have managed to Get It Right by now.

Clearly, many famous personalities in the sporting, entertainment or cultural world fail to be Wallies simply through lack of motivation. Bjorn Borg is a case in point. As a tennis player he was certainly a hard man to beat, but when it came to being a Wally, John McEnroe could wipe the floor with him every time.

A similar case, this time in the field of journalism, is Bernard Levin. The looks and the voice are both highly promising, but when you stop and listen to what the man is actually saying, you realise that he's not merely failing to be a Wally, he's actually going out of his way to avoid being one.

The Levins and the Borgs are hard enough to fathom, but even more exasperating are the ones who teeter on the brink of being Wallies but seem to lack the courage and dedication to go the whole way. The Terry Wogans of this world, for instance, who after years of providing a moderately Wally form of early-morning entertainment and hosting the agreeably Wally Blankety Blank, suddenly go and throw away all chance of being a culture-hero by coming on strong as a compere to an upmarket TV chat show. The Henry Kelly types who one minute are scaling the peaks of Wally achievement on Game For A Laugh and then, next thing you know, are making ill-advised bids for intellectual respectability on the BBC Midweek programme.

The fundamental mistake these people make is to believe that you can somehow try and come over as being thoughtful, rational and articulate and yet retain your credibility as a Wally. It just can't be done.

If you want to appear on, say, Question Time, and still be a Wally, the only way to do it is to abandon all pretence of being thoughtful, rational and articulate and be silly instead.

Not normally Wallies	Frequently Wallies
Eastern mystics*	Post Office clerks
Brain surgeons	Wimbledon line-judges
International tax lawyers	Accordionists
Concert pianists**	Hi-fi buffs
Chess Grand Masters	Tolkein fans
Mastermind champions***	Traffic wardens
International hit men	Radio 1 disc jockeys
Marriage Guidance Counsellors	Former Metropolitan Police Commissioners
Forensic scientists	Train spotters
Financial Times leader writers	Griddle chefs
Polyglots	Darts commentators
Sanskrit scholars	Morris dancers
	Rank Xerox reps
	Figure-skaters
	Rotarians
	Members of the United Nations Security Council
	Buskers
	Fairground barkers
	Cocktail waiters
	Scaffolding contractors
	Town planners
	Taxidermists
	Radio hams
	Railway modellers

Notes

*Eastern mystics. It is possible to be an Eastern Mystic and a Wally *if* you wear a nylon quilted anorak over your robes and distribute leaflets in Oxford Street.

**Concert pianists. Can be Wallies *if* they wear red tuxedos, look pretty, stick to the slow and easy stuff and sign lucrative recording contracts with K-Tel.

Always complete and utter Wallies

Swimming-pool attendants
Motorcycle stunt riders
Demolition derby drivers
Handbell teams
Square-dancing enthusiasts
Jehovah's Witnesses
Headline-writers for the *Sun*
Game-show hosts
Local radio disc jockeys
Druids
Bikers
Nude hang-gliders
Pole-sitters
Roadies
Yodellers
Gurners
Gnomologists
Members of the Sealed Knot
Scientologists/Mormons
Superannuated hippies
Monocyclists
'It's A Knock-Out' teams
Berkshire Tuttimen

Wurzels
Welly-chuckers
Stumblebums
Bicycle jousters
Bollard leapers
Bellyfloppers
The Miss World jury
Flat Earthers
Canary fanciers
Champion pickled egg eaters
Fork-benders
All-in wrestlers
Male models
Members of the Official Raving Monster Loony Party
Loblolly men
Blow Football enthusiasts
Photo-booth nobblers
Bottom pinchers
Balloon dancers
Ticket touts
Beermat collectors

***Obviously, you can be a Mastermind Champion and a Wally if you go on to join the regulars on the BBC Start The Week team.

Further observations
Any Questions hecklers are not necessarily Wallies.

The Maori who exposed his buttocks to the Royal Family but chose the one moment when they were looking the other way was unlucky. He tried to be a Wally and failed.

But since the other panellists are very often being silly too, there's a grave danger that your gesture might pass unnoticed and that you might find yourself being lumped together with the Michael Heseltines, the Willie Whitelaws and the Eric Heffers – people who are not in fact Complete Wallies, just pretty good imitations.

Perhaps all in all it's safest to follow the example of Tony Blackburn, Peter Powell and most successful Wally notables, and resist the temptation to pronounce sagely on world affairs. If you're a true Wally celebrity you should in any case be far too busy opening supermarkets.

HOW TO BE A WALLY ON WHEELS

At first sight, this looks like a pretty daunting topic. Basically, however, it breaks down into two major areas:

1) How to choose a Wally car and equip it with Wally accessories
2) How to drive it like a Wally

The first point all too often gets overlooked by novice Wallies, but it's every bit as important as the second. Lane-hopping or straddling the white line in a less-than-Wally car such as a Fiat Panda is fine as far as it goes. But the danger here is that you could create – as well as exasperation, which of course is the object of the exercise – *confusion* in the minds of other roadusers. They might think, for example, that you've simply had a hard day at the office or that you're on your way back from a Private View or a wine-tasting and that you're being a Wally more or less by accident.

The only way to remove the confusion is both to drive like a Wally and make sure that the car you drive shouts *Wally* loud and clear to every other motorist. This section is intended to help you do both.

But first, a word or two about the mental attitude you will need to adopt towards your car.

If you're a Wally, the very word 'wheels' should be enough to bring you out in goose bumps. It should conjure up a whole world of magically enticing leisure activities brought suddenly within your reach: fascinating one-way systems and intricate spaghetti junctions to explore; famous accident black spots to visit; historic cathedral cities to bypass; and at last that trip up to Coventry to try your hand at ten-pin bowling or see the Barron Knights in cabaret becomes a real possibility!

In the driving seat of your dream on wheels you are no longer just Barry Whatsisname from Accounts who's just been passed over for promotion for the sixth time in as many years – you're a king, a demon, a force to be reckoned with, and your souped-up Capri leaves the boss's boring old Rover standing at the lights every time. Your sex-life looks up, too, when you've got wheels. If you turn up for a date with the average female Wally on nothing more macho than a bicycle, the chances are that you won't get very far. But if you screech to a halt outside her house in a gleaming Escort plastered with Go Faster stripes and dripping with accessories, you'll probably be halfway to putting another notch on your belt before you even get to the front door, and a couple of Snowballs, a Carpenters tape playing softly on the car stereo and a few sotto voce sweet nothings in the car park of the Moon and Parrot will do the rest.

As well as the huge range of exciting things you can do with your motor, there's also the tremendous kick you get simply out of owning it. There's that matchless pride you feel as you run your hand lovingly over the bodywork, playfully fondle the fluffy dice or miniature football boots hanging from the rear-view mirror, or offer the little doggie in the back window his morning bowl of Winalot. Learn to treasure these moments of quiet intimacy between owner and vehicle. They are what being a Wally on wheels is all about.

Which motor?

Learning the complex skills involved in being a Wally driver will always take time and nearly always involve at some point careering off the road and ending up upside down in a field of Brussels sprouts. Choosing a Wally car is a relatively simple matter of paying over the odds for the right credibility-boosting model, and should be painless enough if you follow a few basic guidelines.

First, Wallies *don't* drive Renaults, Citroens, Fiats, Ford Fiestas, Volkswagen Polos, Land Rovers or Range Rovers – or rather, they *can*, but these are not intrinsically Wally marques. Wallies tend to steer clear of foreign makes in general, on the grounds that you can't get the parts. You can of course order the parts from a garage and have them fitted professionally, but it's an important Wally credo that spares hunted down in scrapyards and fitted yourself in your spare time make your car go faster.

The true Wally also scorns the notion of choosing a car on the basis of ease of parking, size of boot, or fuel economy; he sees gas-guzzling, like Black Label-guzzling, as a token of virility. You have probably often heard one Wally say admiringly of another; 'He can't half put it away.' The same principle applies to cars.

So what kind of cars does the discerning Wally go for? It varies according to need. Speed-freak Wallies opt for sporty models that belch out clouds of choking exhaust fumes as they're hammered up to seventy in the Bus Lane, putting the fear of God into other road-users. Wimpier Wallies in trilbies and car coats will probably prefer something more homely – an Morris Marina perhaps: the perfect vehicle in which to chug along and admire the scenery at the head of a three-mile tail-back. Many hard-core auto-enthusiast Wallies plump for cars which never actually move at all, but spend their entire life on bricks in the front garden, while the owner grovels around underneath with a monkey-wrench and a spanner, the object of much ignorant derision from girl-friends, neighbours and passersby.

In general, when buying a car, you should look for the following essential features:

1) An engine with 'poke'
2) Leg-room in the front
3) Leg-over room in the back
4) An ample glove compartment. This makes an excellent home for Man-Size Kleenex Tissues, condoms, Airwicks, back numbers of *Custom Car* and *Auto-Car*, and once a year the envelope containing the £10 note that will see your motor safely through its M.O.T.
5) A large rear window ledge to accomodate fluffy dice, nodding dogs with eyes that light up when you brake, dangling trolls and luminous green spiders, crochet cushions and stereo speakers.
6) A cracked silencer
7) Vast wheel arches, so that you can fit 18-inch

aluminium sports wheels at the back and give your motor that sloping-down-at-the-front look. Also useful for concealing smuggled bottles of Creme de Menthe on your way back from your Continental holiday.

Accessories

To a certain extent, even the non-Wally cars already mentioned could be made to pass as Wally if you equipped them with the right accessories. But only up to a point. A Morris Traveller is never going to look particularly Wally, even if you fur-line the interior and train plastic roses up the timbering.

On a Ford Capri or Cortina, however, you can wreak a really stunning transformation by fitting the following refinements:

1) Autoplas whaletail or quatrofoil boot spoiler
2) Fog lamps with chequered covers
3) Supernumerary brake lights
4) Go Faster stripes
5) Leather or leopard-skin steering wheel glove
6) Musical car horn. Ideally Colonel Bogey, but La Cucaracha, Oh Susannah, Strangers in the Night and the theme tune from The Dukes Of Hazzard will do.
7) Nudge and Roll bars
8) Giant exhaust in gleaming chrome, preferably of the 'bolt-on' variety, *i.e.* serving no practical purpose whatsoever
9) San Francisco number plate
10) Green tinted sunstripe for the windscreen, with your name and your girl-friend's stencilled on it (*unless* you're called Rupert, James, Charles, Sebastian or Julian)

Wally window stickers

The following rear window stickers are valuable Wally credibility-boosters and can safely be fixed to all Wally cars:

- My other car's a Porsche
- This car is a recycled Ferrari
- When God made women drivers he was only joking
- Jim could not fix this
- Happiness is driving over a Traffic Warden's foot
- Passion Wagon – Don't laugh, your daughter may be inside
- 0-60 in 30 minutes
- Don't honk. I'm going as fast as I can, dammit!
- Please pass quietly – driver asleep
- Speed on, brother – Hell ain't half full yet
- This car wants to be a Rolls Royce when it grows up
- Windsurfers do it standing up
- Glider pilots stay up longer
- Rugger players have leather balls
- Only screwing beats canoeing
- Preserve wild life. Pickle a Traffic Warden
- Save energy – Make love slowly

Window stickers that don't belong in Wally cars

1) Any sticker bearing the National Trust oakleaves emblem – an obvious no-no.

2) Green 'Nothing to Declare' stickers. These are used by Volvo drivers as a subtle way of insinuating that they can not only afford an expensive car but an expensive Continental holiday as well. There's therefore not much point in sticking one on a rusting old Ford Zephyr that you picked up for a song via the back pages of your local freesheet.

3) *Caution – show dogs in transit.* Not a Wally sticker unless the dogs in question are Mexican Hairless or Chihuahuas which you're entering for the novelty class.

4) *Carry a kidney donor card.* Borderline. To carry a kidney donor card is exactly the kind of public-spirited act that most Wallies would instinctively avoid. On the other hand, what the sticker also says is '*I* carry a kidney donor card' – and if you think that's going to deter anybody from driving into the back of you, or that anyone is really remotely interested in what you propose to do with your kidneys, you're a Wally.

Guidebooks that don't belong in Wally cars

One kind of book which you will definitely *not* be needing is the expensively produced tome that purports to tell you where to eat 'just off the motorway'. To the true Wally, the willingness of otherwise rational human beings to turn off a motorway and drive for miles down winding pot-holed minor roads, spattering their motor with mud and cow-dung and scratching the paintwork on brambles in search of some dive full of rural geriatrics, is one of the great mysteries of modern times. Many of these so-called pubs do not even serve Black Label and offer nothing more exciting in the way of pub entertainment than a skittle alley out the back and a dartboard with half the stuffing coming out of it. In many of them, too, you can't even stand up straight without knocking your head on some hulking great fourteenth century beam riddled with deathwatch beetle. When a Wally has to pause for refreshment in mid-journey, he eats, drinks and disports himself at the motorway services – or, if he's travelling on a major road, he simply whips out the picnic kit and tucks in by the roadside. You should learn to do the same (see p. 66).

Books with titles such as *The AA/Reader's Digest Treasury of the English Countryside* or *The Hidden Places of Britain* also get a resounding Bronx cheer from Wallies and should not be seen on the back seat of your motor. To a Wally, 'Country' means either John Denver and Dolly Parton, or the dull bits between the towns that aren't lit up at night. He likes urban sprawl, and he's found one or two interesting things to do in Beauty Spots, but in the country he's like a fish out of water. He also finds the silence unnerving.

WAL 1

THE WALLY HIGHWAY CODE

You've now chosen your car. You've paid for it – either with a suitcase full of used notes or by means of a generous loan from Mercantile Credit which you will spend the rest of your natural life trying to repay. You've equipped it with all the accessories – the stickers, the stripes, the dice and so on. Now the time has come for you to venture out on the roads and learn how to be a Sunday driver, not just on Sunday, but *every* day of the week.

This takes practice. Don't be too disappointed if at first you find you can drive to work and back without once mounting the kerb or ploughing into a line of yellow plastic No Parking cones. Stick at it. Eventually you'll find, as thousands of other Wally motorists have found before you, that the ever-present risk of winding up on a Driving Without Due Care and Attention rap, or finding yourself in a mangled heap in the middle of a roundabout on the North Circular, adds that vital extra dimension of motoring enjoyment.

Lane indiscipline. The diagram shows how to achieve very satisfying results by the simple expedient of being in the wrong lane. You're in a left-hand filter lane; the motorists behind naturally assume you're going to *turn* left – yet mysteriously, when the green arrow lights up, you remain stationary. You've had a last-minute change of plan and have decided to go straight on instead. Result: a deafening barrage of honking, effing and blinding from the cars behind.

When the main lights change and the traffic in the right-hand lane begins to move forward, you have two options open to you. You can either (a): suddenly, and without giving any advance warning, veer round to the head of the right-hand queue as if you were overtaking on the inside; or (b): further exasperate the drivers in the left-hand lane by just sitting there like a lemon with your indicator going, waiting until some charitably disposed driver in the right-hand lane decides to stop and let you pull over.

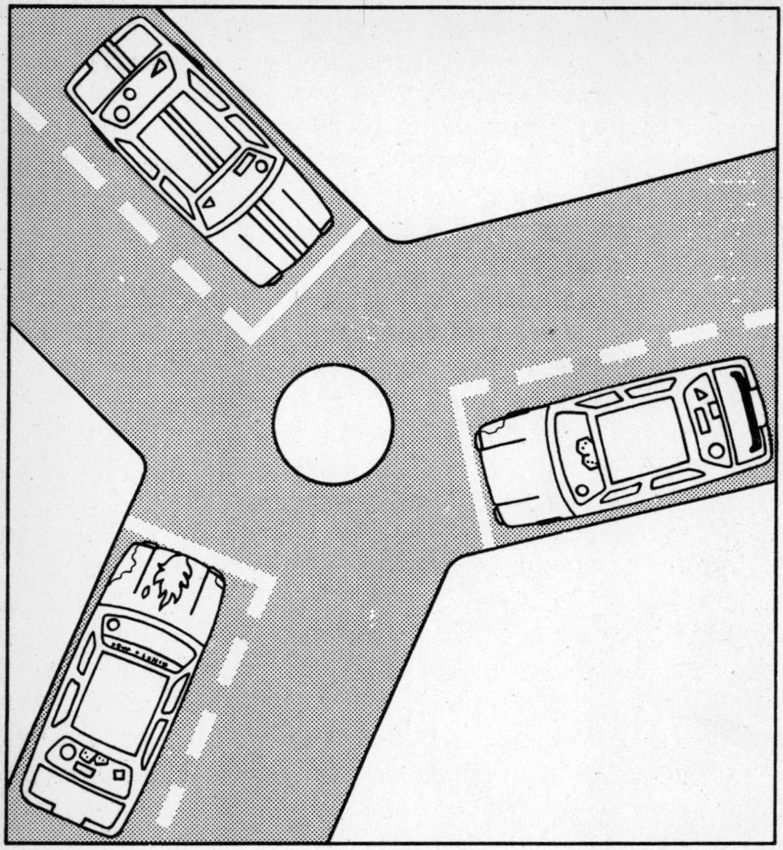

The mini-roundabout. The diagram shows three Wallies at a mini-roundabout. Each is completely baffled by the right-of-way system and is therefore waiting nervously for one of the others to make the first move. What happens next – if anything at all – is anybody's guess. All three could simultaneously make a sudden dash for it and collide in the middle; alternatively, they could stay put for the rest of the afternoon, while huge queues of traffic form behind them in all three directions and the entire traffic system in the surrounding area slowly grinds to a total standstill – in which case, there's the additional benefit that Wallies stranded in the resulting jams will be able to get out of their cars, stretch their legs and brew-up by the roadside. (The adjoining diagram is also available as a novelty drinkmat, entitled 'Still Life').

Overtaking. The only important rule to observe here is that wherever you overtake – on a blind corner, the brow of a hill, or a level crossing – you should afterwards immediately reduce speed until you're going slower than the car you've just overtaken. This is a particularly effective tactic on a narrow or winding road where the other driver has no opportunity to overtake you back.

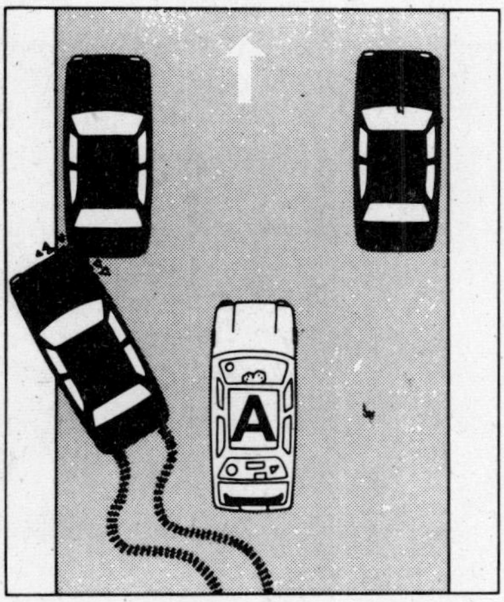

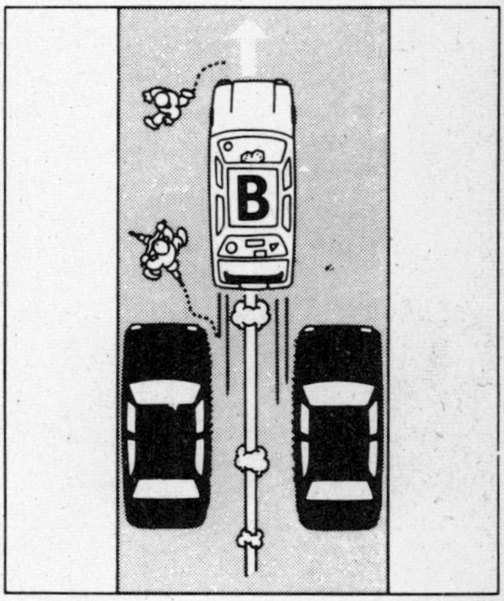

Driving through gaps. An essential skill for the Wally driver is being able to *mis*judge the width of his own car. The two diagrams illustrate in a simplified form how this skill should be applied. Wally A has braked sharply and slowed down to a crawl in order to drive through a gap that would actually take a juggernaut, giving the driver behind such a nasty shock that he's swallowed his dentures and gone careering off the road.

Wally B has gone to the opposite extreme. He has driven at breakneck speed through a gap that he *correctly* judged

to be just that crucial couple of inches too small for his car, ripping the wing mirrors off the stationary vehicles parked on either side, doing appreciable damage to their paintwork and scattering panic-stricken cyclists and pedestrians in all directions.

Either of these two approaches is permissible.

Parking symmetrically. If you're looking for a parking spot in a busy town centre and you're lucky enough to find a spot big enough for *two* cars, try and remember to park exactly in the middle and to leave half a car's length at each end. Leaving a great big gap at one end is asymmetrical and looks messy.

The Pelican crossing. There is always confusion surrounding the exact significance of the flashing orange light on a Pelican crossing. In fact, it's all very simple. The flashing light tells you, the motorist, that if there *are* any pedestrians foolhardy enough to be using the crossing at the time, you are perfectly entitled to run them over. If, on the other hand, there are no pedestrians in sight, *you must stop.* There are, naturally, borderline situations in which you may have to make a difficult choice between putting the wind up pedestrians and annoying the hell out of the driver behind, but in nine cases out of ten it's obvious which course of action is going to get the best results.

Come blow your Colonel Bogey car horn. If you use it to its full potential, your Colonel Bogey car horn can be an instrument of enormous expressive power, capable of conveying a host of different messages. You are *not* getting the most out of it if you simply use it to warn people that you'll drive into the back of them if they don't get out of your way. Other messages include:

Hello Gorgeous
Oi! Don't I know you from somewhere?
I couldn't give a monkey's if this *is* a built-up neighbourhood
Naff off
Last one to the Watford Gap's a Turkey
Just testing.

What to do after a road accident. Look seriously into the whole question of car insurance.

Taking a pride in your motor

One of the great joys of being a Wally on wheels is being able to pile into the motor on a Saturday or Sunday afternoon, zoom off to an area of outstanding natural beauty, pull in at an officially designated picnic site and give those brimming car ashtrays a really thorough clear out. In fact, while you're at it, it's worth giving the whole of the inside of your motor a good going over. You'll be surprised at some of the things you find wedged under the arm rests or under the back seat: fag ends, banana skins and orange peel, half-eaten chips, girlie mags, Kentucky Fried Chicken boxes, crushed Seven-Up cans – it's just amazing how quickly litter accumulates, and if you don't have a purge every couple of weeks or so, you can find yourself driving around in the company of a great reeking pile of waste-paper, cigarette ash and rotting fruit and vegetable matter which can not only pose a serious threat to health but can also impede leg-overs and obstruct your view through the rear windscreen. It doesn't make any kind of sense to let your car get into that kind of state, so do yourself a favour: get rid of the stuff before you catch some horrible disease off it – and if you can find a pleasant spot with a bit of a view in which to go about this frankly rather unpleasant task, and perhaps even have a bit of fun as you scatter it around the countryside, so much the better.

While we're on the subject of beautiful surroundings, it's also worth remembering that no matter how carefully you look after your motor, no matter how much love you give it under the bonnet, there's always a risk that one day it'll develop some terminal mechanical fault and become no longer economic to run. When that day comes, don't prolong the agony unnecessarily: drive or tow it out to a stretch of National Trust parkland, remove the wheels, the fluffy dice, the leopardskin steering wheel glove and anything else that's either still serviceable or that you simply can't bear to part with, and give the poor old banger as dignified a burial as possible, in a stream, pond or clump of trees. It's surely worth risking a paltry fine to know that the motor that gave you so many hours of pleasure is now part of Nature's ever-changing canvas.

One final word of advice. If you're lucky enough to find a ravine to dump it in – don't forget to jump out first.

Before concluding this guide to how to be a Wally on wheels, a brief look at two closely related topics: mopeds and motorbikes; and CB radio.

Mopeds and motorbikes. No very clear guidelines can be laid down here as to what makes are most desirable. *Any* motorbike, moped or even pushbike *can* be Wally if you make it rear up like a Liberty horse and ride it on the back wheel only. However, simply falling off isn't good enough. Anybody can do that.

Don't underestimate these more modest forms of transport. It's surprising how much impact you can make on a quiet suburban cul-de-sac even with a puny Honda 50 if you repeatedly ride it up and down in the small hours of the morning, practising your gear changes. In fact, even if you remain completely stationary and just rev it up in your front garden you can very soon find yourself being voted Public Enemy Number One.

In order to be a real Wally on a motorbike, don't feel you have to go for the 500cc models. 75ccs are ample – better in fact, because the lower the engine capacity, the better the noise-to-performance ratio. The moped is hard to beat in this respect. Even at absurdly low speeds it makes a noise like a bee in a biscuit tin, and the volume increases disproportionately as the needle crawls agonisingly up to the thirty mark. Also, being a Wally on a motorbike is less to do with *what* you ride than the way you ride it. If you think that 75cc of raw power between your legs is going to make you the Barry Sheene of Upper Norwood, you'll be a Wally and no mistake.

CB Radio. CB radio is more than just an accessory in your car – it's an essential. This is not only because it gives you an excuse to stick an enormous aerial on your boot (you ought to have one of those already), but because upwards of 350,000 other Wallies up and down the country are already enthusiastic CB users, and you don't want to get left out. The advantages of CB are obvious. As a Wally Breaker you can:

1) Direct visiting CB-ers to interesting local bottlenecks and recommend greasy spoon roadside diners.
2) Be propositioned by gay long-distance lorry drivers. (If he enquires about the size of your 'rig' or 'thunderstick' suspect the worst.)
3) Receive the very latest up-to-the-minute information on road accidents on your patch. This will enable you to be first on the scene, whip out the emergency warning triangle which up till now has been languishing unused in the back of your car, generally make a bloody nuisance of yourself as police, ambulance and fire-brigade clear away the wreckage and stand around looking officious and public-spirited and congratulating yourself on having played a major role in the rescue effort.

Choice of 'handle'. The first requirement of the Wally CB-er is to adopt a suitable pseudonym or 'handle'. Given the type of handles used by CB-ers – Kinky Knickers, Speedy Lady, Green Gremlin, Twinkle Toes, Bush Baby and so on – it should be obvious that your main problem here is going to be thinking up a daft name that hasn't already been thought of by thousands of other Wallies. If you're really stumped, try one of the following:

Big Girl's Blouse
Simple Simon
Gumboil
Cheeky Chappie
Silly Billy
Butterball
Pimple Bonce
Cloth Ears

Sick Parrot

What the hell do you talk about? Transcripts of conversations between CB-ers reveal that if you're really prepared to work at it, it is possible to drip on literally for hours without once saying anything noteworthy or remarkable. But don't expect to be able to master this skill straight away. For the time being, it'll probably be as much as you can do to select the right frequency without driving into the back of a milk float.

There are two possible approaches to the art of conversing on CB Radio, one very much preferable to the other. The safest way is to stick to topics on which it's virtually impossible to say anything interesting. The other less satisfactory method is to choose potentially interesting topics but to be grindingly dull about them, which tends to require thought. Worse, there's also a risk that you may accidentally let slip some fascinating or blindingly brilliant *aperçu* and suddenly find that your listener has retuned in disgust, leaving you talking into thin air. Topics to avoid include the following:

The active part you take in National Trust fund-raising
Ballet
Batik
Natural Childbirth

THE WALLY AT LARGE

How to be a Wally Consumer

In the eyes of many people, being a Wally shopper is child's play. It's like shoplifting in reverse. All you do is whizz round with your supermarket trolley snatching cheap and nasty items off the shelves more or less at random – things you don't really need at all. Unlike the shoplifter, however, you pay for them on your way out.

Needless to say, there's a great deal more to it than that.

Being a Wally shopper means striking a very careful balance between paying *less* than you ought for essentials such as food, clothing, bedding and furniture and so on – and *more* than you ought for the luxuries: Sodastreams, solenoid-operated cat flaps, electronic door chimes that play Stars and Stripes, and remote-control tellies.

In practice it's not always easy to distinguish between these two categories. A 20 per cent reduction in the price of candlewick loo seat covers at John Lewis can very often persuade you that these are not luxury items at all but essential adornments to your home – which indeed they are if you're a Wally. However, since they're probably still absurdly overpriced for what they are, you're safe to go ahead and buy. Much the same applies to 'bargain' quadrophonic systems, rowing machines, plastic cocktail cabinets in the form of antique globes on castors, and reproduction four-poster beds. Buying *any* of these is bound to up your credibility as a Wally, since whatever the price, it's always going to be too much.

In general, when out shopping, try and observe the following simple rules.

Shop where you see the sign 'Prices Slashed'. This doesn't mean that you should sit down in advance and ask yourself 'What do I need?' and then go out and shop around until you find somewhere that's selling it for a reasonable price – that's exactly the mistake many normal shoppers make. The point is that you should head straight for the signs saying 'Unbeatable bargains' or (surely the five most beautiful words in the English language) 'Buy One, Get One Free', inspect whatever's on offer and somehow convince yourself that you can find a use for it. In nine cases out of ten you'll end up with a product that's still overpriced and that you didn't want or need in the first place.

Look for the free gift. Ideally the freebie should be every bit as desirable as the item actually purchased. *E.g.* a free sherry glass, an E.T. doll or pliable Smurf that melts when you leave it on the radiator, a voucher or coupon which when combined with a ridiculously large number of packet tops or other proofs of purchase, entitles you to a free haircut, a pocket calculator, 30p off the price of a prawn cocktail at a Schooner Inn, a free day's parking in the car park of the Ladbroke Dragonara Hotel, Leeds, or a chance to enter a competition in which you stand a very slim chance indeed of winning two weeks in a cottage overlooking a firing range on Salisbury Plain.*

Look for the hidden defect. Ask yourself: does the product you are about to buy contain a hidden snag that will only become apparent after you've taken it home and thrown away the bag and label? In the case of a garment, this could be a tendency to fall to pieces when exposed to strong sunlight, or to bring on attacks of asthma or hay fever or radiation sickness, or for the colour to drain out in the wash, staining your novelty underpants and 'I choked Linda Lovelace' T-shirt a splendidly eye-catching dayglo orange. If the answer's yes, buy it.

Resist high-pressure sales talk. Shop assistants, particularly in the hi-fi and men's outfitting line, can be very

* However, to bulk-buy a certain brand of washing powder because you get free British Rail travel vouchers with it is not necessarily the act of a Wally. Only if you haven't got a washing machine.

persuasive, and in their frantic eagerness to sell you a product that is very often genuinely worthless and exorbitantly priced, they can sometimes give you the entirely erroneous impression that it may have something going for it after all. In your disappointment at finding that it's not the complete waste of money you were banking on, you will then lose interest, walk out of the shop – and kick yourself later when you realise you missed a once-in-a-lifetime opportunity to pay good money for a first-class load of old rubbish.

Shops No Wally Should be Seen Dead In

Antiquarian Booksellers. Wally reading matter is bought at newsagents and tobacconists along with Mars Bars, fags and plastic combs. If you want a book with that well-thumbed look, the place to go is the bargain racks at Susan Reynolds.

Health Food Shops. As a Wally you should be able to break wind wherever and whenever the occasion demands without the help of red kidney beans, lentils, brown rice or other aids to flatulence.

Interflora. Wallies don't say it with flowers – at least, not real ones. If you want to show her you care, send her a bad taste greetings card from John Menzies or, for special occasions, a Wallygram. This where three Wallies in football scarves turn up on her doorstep and spray her with beer from a Party Four.

The Waitrose on the King's Road. Shopping in a supermarket that sells fresh Fennel, Ochra and Calabrise can seriously damage your Wally credibility.

Christian Bookshops. For you, inspirational literature means *101 Uses of a Dead Cat*.

Buying through classified ads. One of the secrets of being a Wally shopper lies in avoiding simply buying second-rate or shoddy goods and in knowing where you can lay your hands on goods that are shoddy, second-rate and Wally too. This is where the Under a Fiver column of your local newspaper or freesheet can come in handy. A typical week's offerings usually include: Draylon seat covers in a variety of exciting shades; multi-coloured ex-Bed and Breakfast nylon sheets to snag your toenails on; clapped-out Music Centres; china carthorses; Bri-nylon housecoats; assorted carpet squares – all on offer at a give-away £4.99.

Items of bed linen or clothing purchased through an Under a Fiver column should be approached with extreme caution, preferably while wearing full protective clothing and should on no account be handled until they have been left to soak for several days in a bath containing a powerful industrial cleansing agent. This should remove stubborn stains and all but the very hardiest forms of insect or fungal life.

Shopping by mail. Shopping by mail involves an element of risk which should appeal to your sporting instincts. You never know quite what you're going to end up with. You could order a gilt carriage clock and be sent a cartwheel spice rack; you could order a Wellington boot tidy and end up with a hostess trolley. Alternatively, the mail order company to whom you've just sent a substantial cheque could suddenly cease trading and mysteriously vanish off the face of the earth. The next thing you know, there they are, featured in an hilarious item on That's Life.

How to buy a sumptuous hand-crafted Objet D'art which you will be proud to display in your home and cherish for all time. One of the most obvious ways to show that you're a Wally consumer is to send off for one of the numerous commemorative collectors' items advertised in colour supplements and glossy magazines.

On the face of it, nothing could be more straightforward. You just fill in the tear-off order form, enclose a cheque for a colossal sum of money, stick it in the post, and hey presto, within twenty-eight days, along comes your immaculately tooled African Wild Life lamp-base – a miracle of craftsmanship and life-like detail which will survive to grace your home long after the various endangered species represented on it have disappeared off the face of the earth, turned into fur coats, hearth rugs, waste-paper baskets and ivory figurines for other Wallies to squander their money on.

Of course, buying a timeless artefact isn't quite as easy as all that. Stop and think about it for a moment. If it *was* that easy, everybody would be doing it. And if everybody was sending off for Royal Wedding Teaspoon Sets, they wouldn't be collectors' items any more.

The catch is this. In order to reach the cheque-book-at-the-ready stage, you must sincerely believe that the artefact that you are about to buy has been hand-made in the traditional way by Europe's finest master-craftsmen, using techniques handed down over the centuries – and *not* mass-produced in Stoke on Trent or turned out by sweated labour somewhere in the Third World.

In practice it takes a special breed of Wally to pull off such an astonishing feat of credulity.

So how do you, a novice, bridge the gullibility gap?

One relatively painless method is to read through the sample order form on p. 60 and practise signing your name at the bottom until you feel credulous enough to tackle the real thing.

ORDER FORM FOR SUMPTUOUS HAND-CRAFTED OBJET D'ART

Please enter with all possible speed my order for this superb

☐ Onyx table lighter
☐ Porcelain figure of Italian boy in straw hat
☐ Two-handed Anglo-Saxon cider quaffer
☐ 18th century oxo-cube dispenser
☐ Set of ornamental brass dildos
☐ Queen Anne fondue set

which has been produced to commemorate

☐ The War of Jenkyns' Ear
☐ The Raising of the *Mary Rose*
☐ The sinking of the *Belgrano*
☐ The 500th Glorious Year of *The Mousetrap*
☐ The Relief of Mafeking
☐ The International Year of the Wally

and contains a tastefully inset

☐ Pre-decimal threepenny bit
☐ Fragment of the True Cross
☐ Piece chipped off Stonehenge

I understand that this/these sublime artefact(s) has/have been

☐ Hand-painted by trained chimpanzees on the finest bone china,
☐ Richly bordered with 22 carat gold which will in no circumstances come off in my dish-washer,

and I look forward to receiving with it/them a Certificate of Authenticity attesting to its/their unique qualities and pointing out that if for any reason I am not satisfied with it/them, it is now too late to get my money back. I need not sent a cheque now. I understand that I will be invoiced immediately prior to the despatch of my SUMPTUOUS HAND-CRAFTED OBJET, by which time the price will have doubled. I also solemnly undertake not to complain and make a fuss when I discover that my SUMPTUOUS HAND-CRAFTED OBJET is only half the size of the one shown in the advert.

Name A. Wally ....

Camping out for the January Sales

Camping out for the January Sales is a traditional Wally activity and an essential feature of the post-Christmas scene. But it can be dangerous and shouldn't be attempted by anyone who isn't in absolutely peak physical condition. At that time of year, those Oxford Street pavements can be mighty chilly, especially at night. Also, there are all kinds of problems involved in camping in a built-up area, particularly when you're liable to discover that all the nearest loos and telephone boxes are out of action because you vandalised them on your last trip up to the West End.

When queueing for the Sales, you will need:

1) Grappling irons
2) Pile ointment
3) Water divining rod
4) Shotgun, primed and loaded, to keep by your side at all times
5) A silly hat or enormous stripey scarf or giant teddy bear
6) Hunting knife strapped to your leg for close combat
7) Also, nowadays more and more people are giving sale-queueing a bad name by taking advantage of media publicity to promote deserving causes, or getting other people to sponsor them for every day they spend in the queue and donating the proceeds to charity. In order to dissociate yourself from these kind of antics, it's a good idea to take along a large placard making clear that you're in it purely for personal gain

Nobody said that being a Wally is all fun. Spending up to a week in a sleeping bag outside a department store certainly isn't. Nor is it like any camping holiday you've ever experienced. For a start, instead of being woken by the sound of cattle lowing in the adjoining meadow or Frenchmen clearing their nasal passages in the campsite washrooms, you're more likely to find yourself being kicked or prodded awake by muggers and vagrants demanding money with menaces, accidentally trampled by Hare

The Wally Imaginary Guitar Tutor

Yes, being a guitar hero is easy thanks to this step-by-step guide. *And you don't have to play a note*!

- No more poring over chord charts!
- No more painful callouses on the ends of your fingers!
- Astound your friends at Status Quo concerts!

Just stick a heavy metal album on the turntable of your Music Centre, turn the volume up full blast, and strain, strut, groan and grimace your way through these exciting poses and lurid facial contortions.

1 The Opening Stance

2 The Real Heavy Number

3 The Squealing Guitar Solo

4 The Splits

5 The Total Flake-out

Facial Contortions

Krishna monks assembling for the first chant of the day, or greeted by a dawn chorus of jeers, catcalls and hoots of derision from dustmen, taxi-drivers and office cleaners on the early shift. Of course, it's all part of the experience – but it can be alarming if you're not expecting it.

Apart from all the more obvious unpleasantnesses, you should also be aware of two other potential hazards.

Nobbling. If you join a sale queue expecting cosy sing-songs round the campfire and a comradely 'We're all in this together' spirit, you're in for a nasty shock. All that stuff is strictly for the TV cameras. The truth is that even in daylight hours the atmosphere of simmering rivalry in a sale queue is something frightening; after the sun goes down and the shadows begin to lengthen, it's downright terrifying. When the doors are thrown open and those bargain-hungry punters stampede through into the store it's going to be every man for himself – and everybody in the queue knows it. The queue member who lets you borrow his copy of *Dalton's Weekly* one day could slit your throat for a place at the glassware counter the next.

So when you wake up in the mornings and you've managed to rub some of the circulation back into your aching limbs, *don't* go trying to curry favour by passing round your thermos and Benzedrine tablets; just be grateful that nobody from further down the queue has come round in the middle of the night and tried to remove your arms and legs with a machete.

Queue fatigue. After a few days' queueing, even the most fastidious type is going to look pretty much of a wreck: hair greasy and lifeless and impregnated with soot and exhaust fumes, eyes red through lack of sleep, three days' growth of beard ... Some of the men will look fairly unprepossessing too. Be prepared for this, and *don't* go with unrealistic hopes of perhaps striking up some kind of relationship with a female queue-member. Most of the women you meet in sale queues probably won't be your type anyway – they're usually the kind that can turn the bathtaps on and off just by scowling at them.

The joy of supermarket trolley cruising

Jumping over rows of double-decker buses on a motorbike or leaping out of hot-air balloons and dangling by your ankles from lengths of knicker elastic can be fun, but unfortunately they both involve a bit of advance planning – and that means they're beyond the scope of all but a few very dedicated Wallies.

Cruising around in a supermarket trolley, though, is something *all* Wallies can and should have a go at. It doesn't involve any prior organisation, it's just as enjoyable – and it's free.

This is not to say that it's entirely without risk. Goodness knows, it's hard enough pushing a trolley around Tesco's when all it's got in it is a pair of Bachelor's Cup-A-Soups, a pre-cooked Lasagne for two and a packet of chicken drumsticks. It's *doubly* hard when you're wrestling to control a runaway trolley containing two or perhaps even three Wallies, all of them singing at the tops of their voices, waving football scarves and scattering empty crisp packets and Dr Pepper cans in all directions.

Unless you're dead set on winding up in the casualty department, it pays to follow a few simple precepts.

1) If you're going to be a passenger, remember to remove the shopping first. Sitting perched for any length of time on top of a frozen turkey can adversely affect your sex-life – quite apart from which, it's very annoying to discover later when unpacking your purchases that you've got a dozen broken eggs and two packets of crushed Waffles on your hands.

2) Try to resist the temptation to trolley-cruise down the ramps of multi-storey carparks. These are reserved for Wallies in cars pretending to be Starsky and Hutch, and the speeds they get up to on those blind corners can be quite frightening.

3) Up to a point, the unpredictability of a supermarket trolley is what gives it its charm. But for God's sake, if you're the one who's pushing, and you're on a slope, *don't let go*. Those little castors on the front have got a

mind of their own, and if you're not careful you could find yourself watching helplessly as trolley and human cargo crash through a barrier and disappear down a hole in the road or go hurtling through the plate-glass window of the nearest TV rental showroom. This could not only seriously damage the health of the passengers, it could also ruin the enjoyment of the crowd of Wallies on the pavement outside watching Celebrity Golf from Gleneagles.

Roadside picnicking

Like so many Wally activities, roadside picnicking is by no means as easy as it looks and should not be regarded as a form of recreation or relaxation.

One of the first problems you will have to contend with is that of struggling to erect recalcitrant picnic tables and folding stools while being buffeted by the tailwind from passing juggernauts. For the same reason, you're also going to have a devil of a job keeping that primus stove alight. A windbreak of the kind used on beaches can sometimes offer limited protection but it's often hard work trying to hammer the wooden stakes through four inches of unyielding tarmac.

Once your kettle has finally boiled, your tea has brewed and you've managed to unpack the tuna fish rolls from their layers of cling-film, you then face the problem of removing your oxygen mask for long enough to eat them while at the same time managing not to be overcome by exhaust fumes – which can be quite a feat of brinkmanship.

Ignore people who jeer at you from passing cars. They've probably never tried it themselves and haven't the faintest notion of the problems involved.

Two safety tips: always leave a margin of at least three feet between your picnic table and the nearest thundering oil tanker, and *don't* go in for brightly coloured tablecloths in jazzy designs that could startle motorists or flap around and get caught in the wheels of passing cars. This could cause a serious accident which could completely take away your appetite and even force you to abandon the picnic altogether. What's more, you'd never get the creases out of the tablecloth.

Where to picnic. Unfortunately, many of the really challenging and spectacular picnic spots are off-limits for one reason or another. The elevated section of the M4 is really just a bit too exposed for comfort – a sudden fierce gust of wind here could spell disaster, scattering your Ryvita and Primula cheese spread, and possibly you too, over half of Brentford. The same goes for the otherwise magnificent stretch of the M6 north of Junction 15 – with the additional hazard that thick fog mixed with diesel smoke from lorries grinding their way up that long incline can reduce visibility drastically and turn even the simplest task, such as finding your way to the liver sausage sandwiches or remembering where you put the picnic mustard, into a major trauma.

Large roundabouts, particularly if attractively landscaped and planted out with floral clocks, can make an ideal venue for a roadside picnic, and it's surprising that they're so little exploited by Wallies. However, if picnicking on a roundabout, do make sure you go fully prepared. There's nothing more frustrating than risking life and limb weaving your way through three fast-moving lines of traffic while laden down with chairs, table, primus stove and insulated picnic box, only to discover on arrival that you've forgotten the tin-opener.

Practice makes perfect. Like most high-visibility Wally activities, roadside picnicking should not be attempted until you're fully aware of all the potential risks and you're sure in your own mind that the project's not going to go off at half-cock, *i.e.* that you're *not* going to find yourself downwind of a Port-A-Loo used by gangs of Irish labourers in donkey jackets, or upstaged by a party of hitch-hikers or a hot-dog stand. You should also take precautions against being mistaken for a member of an avant-garde theatre group making a statement about environmental pollution and so get carted off by the police.

The best thing is to start modestly by practising in a car park – ideally an underground or multi-storey one where you're protected from the elements but also exposed to hefty doses of carbon monoxide. From there, work up to 'B' roads, building up confidence every time, until finally you're ready to tackle your first main roads and dual carriageways.

It will take time, but think of the rewards.

GET IT DOWN YOU

The Wally Good Drink Guide

Being a Wally can be extremely thirsty work, and after a hard day starting a forest fire or hogging the roundabouts in a children's playground, there's nothing more refreshing than to saunter into the Captain's Bar of the Moon and Parrot, order a pint of deliciously full-bodied Black Label, and chuck it over your best friend. He will then return the compliment by chucking one all over you, and before you know it everybody else will be joining in and the evening will have got off to a flying start.

Many novice Wallies make the elementary mistake of thinking that all you can do with drink is Get It Down you by the gallon. This is being very unimaginative. You can also Get It Down other people by pouring it over them from a tankard or spraying it at them out of a can (see p. 75). You can Bring It Up in interesting patterns either in the car park of the pub, on the pavement outside your local Pro Nuptia, or at home in your avocado vanity unit. And the following night as you return to the Moon and Parrot and set about going for the double, you can also Bring It Up Again – metaphorically this time, by entertaining friends or even total strangers with a blow-by-blow account of your antics the night before, going over the whole proceedings literally *ad nauseam.*

Before going on to discuss what to drink and where to drink, a few myths and common misconceptions about Wally drinking habits need to be discussed.

First, let's be clear about one thing. You shouldn't actually *need* strong alcoholic drink in order to go out and put the boot into a telephone box, wrap yourself round a lamp-post, or filch a collection of Road Up signs to decorate your bedroom. If you know your stuff you should be able to manage all those things quite comfortably on half a pint of Barbican. It's simply that because you're a Wally, you *like* the sensation of having six pints of lager, three whisky chasers and a couple of brandies for the road all slopping around in the pit of your stomach.

Secondly, it's not a good idea to pay too much attention to the killjoys who tell you that with every nip of own-brand supermarket Scotch, a million of your desperately needed brain cells will bite the dust. If you want to get the matter in perspective, remember that ten minutes' exposure to Good Morning Britain will probably dispose of at least twice as many – and for a fraction of the fun.

Most traditional drink guides approach the matter very much from the point of view of the drinker. But as we've seen, there are a number of other exciting things you can do with it as well. What follows, then, is a necessarily brief look at various tipples from the point of view of the drinker, pourer, chucker, sprayer and chunderer.

Beer. A vast range to choose from here, with many regional variations. Bear in mind, though, that the ones that get you in a window-smashing mood aren't always the ones with the best pouring or spraying properties – nor do they always give the best adhesion on lino floors. The best way to find the one that suits you is to experiment by chucking a wide selection, starting with the fizzy kegs and working your way steadily round to the dark, treacly Newcastle Browns, Old Peculiars and Winter Warmers at the other end of the spectrum. Stick with – if you'll forgive the pun – whichever one you feel most happy with. If you find you can stomach the taste too, you're home and dry – which is a great deal more than you can say for the people you've chucked it over.

A word here about the Campaign for Real Ale. CAMRA is chocker with Wallies, as you'd expect, and certainly if you're not a Wally when you join, by the time you've met the other members, developed a florid complexion and giant beer gut and spent a few evenings discussing the specific gravity of obscure West Country bitters while lying horizontal on the sawdust strewn floor of a Real Ale pub, you very soon will be.

However, not all Wallies are die-hard Real Ale enthusiasts by any means. Many feel that if you're going to drink beer that's flat, cloudy and has lots of unsavoury-looking bits floating in it, the proper thing to do is to save yourself a few pennies and brew it yourself.

Lager. Lager is the Wally drink *par excellence*, but choosing the right brand from all the Heinekens, Hemelings, Carlings, Stellas and so on can be a real problem. The ads don't help here. Amongst all those tankards bursting out of blocks of ice in slow motion, humanoid bears relaxing at the local and ordering drinks all round, and rugged-looking types in denim shirts striding purposefully across sun-parched deserts, there's not one that tells the Wally punter what he wants to know about the product, *i.e.* what harmful chemical additives does it contain? How long has it been kept festering in a plastic vat? Will it do lasting damage to your insides? And so on.

Perhaps the marketing men are afraid that if they revealed that it wasn't brewed in steaming wooden tubs by Vikings but by spotty little men in white coats in places like Slough, they'd lose sales. If so, one can only say that they sadly underestimate the brand loyalty of Joe Wally down at the Moon and Parrot.

If you want to be a discerning Wally drinker, don't allow sophisticated television advertising campaigns to interfere with your choice of lager. Just work your way systematically through the major brands until you find the one that makes you burp the loudest and tastes most reminiscent of chilled horse pee.

Sherry. Not a drink for any Wally concerned with establishing his credibility among his mates. This is the kind of drink your bank manager might offer you before refusing your request for extended overdraft facilities. Buy your girl-friend a Sweet Sherry as an aperitif in a Berni, but otherwise avoid.

Wines and spirits. Lack of volume and expense are the two main drawbacks here, so there isn't much you can do with either type except drink them – which makes them dull for the Wally. The trouble is, they come in such miserable little glasses. Chucking a gin and tonic down the back of someone's neck may be a good laugh, but at upwards of 90p a time it's certainly not a cheap one. Also, in order to produce any kind of satisfactory reaction you're going to have to jettison the whole glass, gin, tonic, ice and lemon and all. You could theoretically just give your victim the ice and the tonic and retain the rest, but it could earn you a reputation for being stingy, especially when other Wallies are slopping pints around.

Another drawback is that few wines and spirits can be shaken up in the bottle and squirted. The only fizzy drinks in this line are the sparkling whites, the Lambruscos and the Champagnes, and since there's nothing you can do with any of them that you can't do just as enjoyably and effectively with a can of Skol, it seems pointless going to all that extra expense – on top of which, people might think you were being ostentatious.

Soft drinks. Certain drinks become Wally when sprayed over passersby; others are intrinsically Wally even before they leave the can. In other cases, such as Coke, Wally status isn't fully assured until the empty can has been dropped into someone's front garden or run over by a car. The following, however, can be sipped out of the finest crystal goblets and will still be Wally: Fanta (any flavour), Dr Pepper, Schweppes Cariba, Top Deck Lemonade Shandy, Seven-Up, Pineapple and Grapefruit Lilt, Tizer, Corona, Robinson's Passionade, Diet Pepsi, Bingo Cola.

Drinks for the Harlow Harpie and other female Wallies. The female Wally has an exasperating fondness for exotic and usually expensive concoctions such as Ponies, Snowballs, White Ladies, Crocodillos, Riccadonnas, Rum and blackcurrant, Creme de Menthe, Port and lemonade, Campari and soda – although you may be lucky and find one who drinks nothing but Slimline tonic.

Be warned: cocktails are also a favourite. Many Wally pubs have a so-called Happy Hour when you can buy them at half-price, but they're still not exactly cheap. If you can shell out a fiver on a round of Pinacoladas and Harvey

Wallbangers and manage to look happy, have no fear – you're definitely a Wally.

Where to drink – the Wally Pub Guide

Choosing the right pub is crucial. There's nothing worse than striding confidently into what you imagine to be a Wally pub only to find yourself surrounded by bearded Radio Three listeners earnestly discussing late Bartok, trendies in granny specs and fisherman's smocks reviving ancient and deservedly neglected pub games from the Black Country, and finger-in-the-ear folk singers wearing Arran sweaters or sheepskin jerkins performing incomprehensible songs about obscure mining disasters. It's bad enough when you're on your own: it's potentially disastrous if you're with a group of other Wallies who up till now have respected you for your general taste and discernment. Bang goes your Wally credibility.

There are pubs for folkies and domino-players, and there are pubs for people like you. You stay off their patch, they'll stay off yours. The rule is: only drink in Wally pubs, *unless* (a) you are deliberately venturing into non-Wally territory in order to conduct some kind of public relations exercise on behalf of Wallies, such as a demonstration of beer-chucking, crisp-packet bursting or peanut-juggling; or (b) you are in possession of a six-pack of Heineken or some such, in which case you are free to drink more or less anywhere you like. In fact, the more imaginative your choice of location the better. *Don't* just sit at home and swill it down in front of The Professionals – take a couple of cans and experiment with different venues: squatting on the pavement outside Sainsbury's; stretched out on a gravestone; or if you can afford it, sprawled across four seats of a British Airways passenger flight to Malta.

How to find a Wally pub. Experienced Wallies can sniff out Wally pubs in the most unlikely places. You'll find it harder to begin with. Basically, though, it's not so much a question of where to look as of what to look for. To avoid making embarrassing mistakes which could lead your friends to question your nous and put unnecessary strain on your bottle, give any likely-looking pub a brief once-over first, asking yourself the following questions:

1) Does it contain a huge Alsatian fed on dropped crisps and half-eaten ploughman's lunches?
2) Does it offer the very latest in pub entertainment? (*I.e.*, table video games: Asteroids, Astro-Blasters, Space Invaders; a jukebox that plays The Human League an average of fifteen times per session; Friday night guest appearances by Country and Western artistes who, according to the poster, have appeared regularly on TV but who in fact have never appeared regularly anywhere except in the Engagements Wanted columns of the *Melody Maker*.)
3) Does it contain blackened roof timbers bearing the sign 'Duck or Grouse'?
4) Are the toilets labelled 'Guys and Dolls', 'Cocks and Hens', 'Actresses and Bishops', or 'Lords and Ladies'?
5) Are the walls of the Gents covered with graffiti painstakingly copied from paperbacks by Nigel Rees? Does it also contain a contraceptive machine on which someone has scribbled 'Buy me and stop one' or 'This chewing gum tastes revolting'?
6) Is there a parrot or minah bird behind the bar that squawks 'Time, gentlemen, please'?

While you're at it, it's also worth finding out – assuming it's not abundantly clear already – whether or not the landlord is a Wally too. The Wally landlord usually exhibits the following characteristics:

1) He is a former heavyweight boxing coach or record producer who has worked with all the big names in the business.
2) He sucks up to members of the local constabulary by inviting them to discreet naughty-naughty after-hours drinking sessions with the regulars.

The Wally Step by Step Guide to Drinking from Ring-Pull Cans

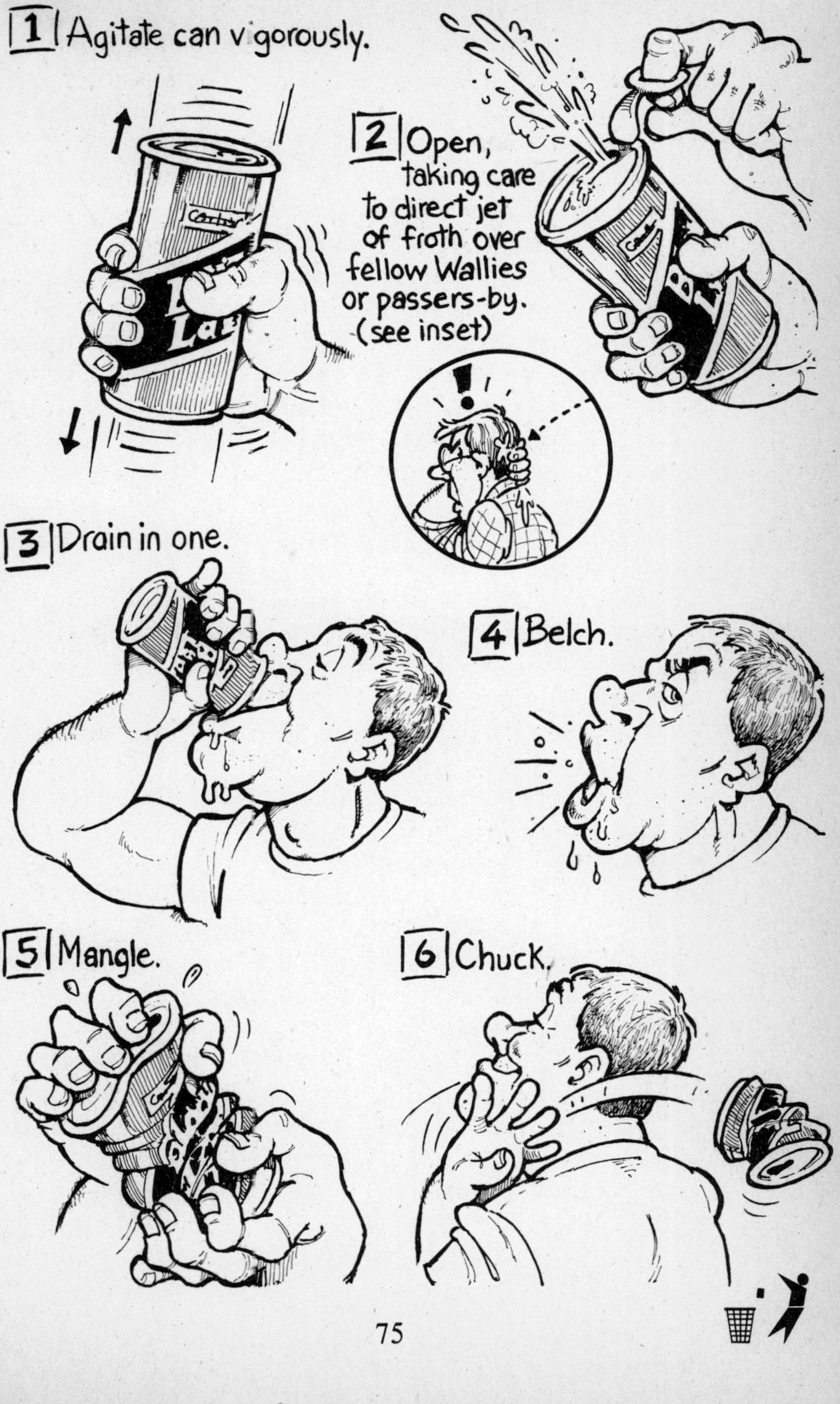

3) He sends departing patrons on their way with a cheery 'Don't forget the seat belts'.
4) He not only welcomes passing trade in the form of parties of middle-aged ladies in crimplene trouser suits and cowboy hats; he lies down in the middle of the road in the path of oncoming coaches and implores them to pull in and taste his internationally famous bar snacks.
5) He festoons the walls with postcards sent by regulars holidaying in Majorca and photographs bearing warm messages of friendship from (a) famous people he crawled to in his heavyweight boxing or record-producing days, or (b) hapless celebrities who once made the mistake of sneaking into his pub to use the toilets and found they couldn't get back to their car without signing autographs and buying drinks all round.

Wally pub grub

There are strict rules governing the serving of food and bar snacks in Wally pubs and it's up to you as a Wally consumer to see that standards are maintained. Don't buy food from pubs where the following rules are not observed:

1) Practically everything except soup should be served in a basket.
2) Where possible, food should induce halitosis. Salads should be heavy on the spring onions and ploughman's lunches should always be accompanied by more Branston pickle, piccallilli and pickled onions and cocktail gherkins than anyone except a bad-breath fanatic would want to eat.
3) Sandwiches should be left to mature in the kitchens for several days and allowed to make their own way to the food counter, where they should then be garnished with a sprig of fresh parsley and smothered in Clingfilm.
4) All bar and kitchen staff should be issued with Photofit pictures of Egon Ronay and local Department of Health inspectors and trained in case of emergency to

activate a self-destruct mechanism concealed beneath the food counter.

5) Pub diners who make a nuisance of themselves by changing their order at the last minute or losing their cloakroom ticket should either be verbally ridiculed in front of other customers or have soup spilt down them.

6) Quiche Lorraine, if available, should be referred to on the menu as 'flan'.

7) Items of confectionery should be on sale behind the bar. Crisps should be available in as many outlandish flavours as possible – Roast Ox, Prawn Cocktail, Barbecued Piranha Fish – but never the one you actually ask for.

8) All Scotch eggs should contain a gap of approx. 1/8 in. between the egg and the sausage meat, and the breadcrumbs should on no account be crisp.

THE W-PLAN DIET

If you want to be a Wally, you've got to eat like a Wally.

There's no way you can seriously contemplate a busy day's welly-chucking or poster defacement on a meagre diet of starch-reduced crispbread, unsweetened orange juice, black coffee and the odd slice of raw carrot. You need something considerably more substantial.

What you need is the W-Plan Diet.

The W-Plan Diet consists of solid, no-nonsense, no-nutritional-value junk food that catapults you straight into the coronary high-risk bracket and will have you wearing false teeth by thirty.

The W-Plan Diet is tailor-made to meet the varied needs of today's busy go-anywhere perpetual-motion Wally. It doesn't involve boring calorie charts and long lists of dietary dos and don'ts; it doesn't require you to gulp down huge quantities of grapefruit with every meal or make a complete social leper of yourself by living only on All Bran or rabbit food. With the W-Plan Diet you eat what you like, where you like, when you like: Benson's Kingsnax, Planter's Peanuts, French bread pizzas, chip butties, Angel Delight, whatever you fancy – so long as it comes in a brightly coloured wrapper, you can stuff it down you.

Flexibility is the keynote. Instead of laying down the law about what you can and can't eat, the W-Plan Diet is *realistic* about your eating habits. It recognises that there may be times when you have no choice but to eat a slice of wholemeal bread. It says: if you *have* to, go ahead – but at least try and kill the taste by spreading it with Ham and Cheese Toasties, or cancel out the effect by having an extra helping of Alphabetti Spaghetti later in the day.

There are really only two rules you should bear in mind when following the W-Plan Diet.

1) If you have to cook food yourself, at least keep preparation time to a minimum. As a Wally, you've got better things to do than sit in your knotty-pine kitchen with your eyes glued to an oven-timer. Stick to foods that

you can boil in the bag, bung in a microwave oven or serve simply by adding hot water.
2) Try and eat your meals with the telly on. This applies particularly to breakfast. Even devilled kidneys and kedgeree can be part of your W-Plan Diet if you eat them while watching Breakfast Television.

W-Plan menus for special occasions

Choosing the right menu for that intimate soiree can be something of a problem, not only for beginners but even for the veteran Wally host and hostess. What dishes are and are not Wally?

The answer very much depends on the way they're prepared and served and the exact circumstances in which they're eaten. Braised duckling with olives served with new potatoes, artichoke hearts and a side-salad is not exactly traditional Wally fare – but you could make it acceptable if you drowned it in brown sauce and expected your guests to shovel it down with a couple of slices of Mother's Pride and a cup of PG Tips while watching Crossroads. Similarly, Gateau Mille Feuilles au Citron: not an item gracing many Wally dinner tables – but you might just smuggle it past an undiscerning palate if it was cunningly smothered in tinned custard or Bird's Dream Topping.

Other cases are even less clear-cut. Caviare, for example. Could it be Wally if you served it in a toasted sandwich? Would Chocolate Bath Oliver biscuits be Wally if you got a free voucher with every tin entitling you to send away for a cut-price Swiss Army pen-knife? Hard to say.

What *is* clear is that initially at least, success as a Wally chef depends on going by the book and avoiding risky flights of culinary fancy until you've mastered the basics. More experienced Wally cooks can take even the most unappetising-sounding dishes and transform them into something really special: tasting their Moussaka or Baked Alaska you'd almost swear you were eating a Fray Bentos steak and kidney pie or a shop-bought Arctic Roll. For you, it's more important to concentrate on simple menus. Try and remember too those little details that are so vital to successful Wally cuisine.. There's nothing more discouraging than to go to endless trouble preparing a slap-up banquet consisting of frankfurters in brine and a dollop of Smash followed by fruit cocktail and Ideal milk, only to see the entire evening ruined because you failed to bring on the Branston or make with the after-dinner mints.

Enlivening your W-Plan Diet

One exciting way to inject variety into your diet is to try eating out at home once in a while. It sounds like a contradiction in terms, but it *can* be done if you follow the instructions and sample menus set out below.

The Stay-At-Home British Airways In-Flight Ham Salad Banquet for 1. Holidays come all too rarely – so why not relive all the excitement of starting out on a two-week package tour of the Costa Brava, only this time without setting foot outside your own front door?

Simply draw the curtains of your lounge-diner, litter the room with mementos of the trip or screen some holiday home movies to get yourself in the mood, then strap yourself into your Parker Knoll recliner – and it's chocks away!

Without waiting for smoking or seatbelt restrictions to be lifted, pour yourself a plastic tumbler of Bacardi, tear open a carton of those duty-free Winstons you put by specially for the occasion and light up. While a friend or loved one violently agitates your easy chair to simulate in-flight turbulence, tuck into those glistening squares of processed ham, tired-looking lettuce leaves, cocktail gherkins, Jacob's Cream Crackers with squidgy semi-melted butter, and jellied pears with angelica on the top. Round off your meal by spilling scalding hot coffee in your lap as your companion announces that due to a strike by Spanish air traffic controllers your flight has been diverted to Zurich.

Variation: As above, except that you simulate the return flight. This involves less outlay on food: you're suffering from gastro-enteritis and all you can eat are Cream Crackers.

The In-Flight Ham Salad Banquet for 1

The Stay-At-Home Berni Inn on Cup Final Night Special. However much you'd like to, it's just not possible to dine at a Berni Inn every night of the week. So once in a while why not do the next best thing and try and recreate that unique Berni ambience in your own front room? It's cheap, easy – and if you're going all out for authenticity, you could even arrange for a group of your Wally friends to burst in halfway through the meal and impersonate a jubilant horde of victorious Manchester United fans chucking bread rolls and yelling for service.

Prepare the scene by spreading red chequered tablecloths over everything in sight and pour a brimming tankard of Black Label for yourself and a huge schooner of sweet sherry for your female companion while the two of you study the menu. One of you should then take the role of waiter or waitress, while the other, after hours of thought, finally opts with devastating originality for prawn cocktail followed by steak and chips; whoever is acting the customer then has all the fun of sending back the steak when it arrives either toasted to a crisp or stone cold in the middle. As fitting end to a perfect evening, you should then stage a pointless argument over the bill and storm out, having first filled your pockets with bread rolls and miniature packs of butter, leaving the waiter/waitress to be roasted on a spit by those Manchester United fans who are not already fully occupied performing Tommy Cooper tricks with the tablecloths.

The Stay-At-Home Motorway Service Station breakfast. As any true Wally will tell you, there's nothing quite like staggering red-eyed with exhaustion into the Watford Gap Services after six hours' night driving and tucking into a high-cholesterol breakfast of chips, beans, fried egg and bacon and toast and jam, especially when you can eat within earshot of the Space Invaders and relax to the sound of a heavy metal band and their road crew, fresh from a gig, thrashing hell out of a pinball machine outside – and that's the experience you can recreate in your own home thanks to this unique Wally Stay-At-Home.

Simply stock up in advance with plastic tubs of butter

and jam and cook all food the previous night. Leave to stew overnight on a hostess trolley; then in the morning invite a party of headbangers or long-distance lorry drivers to share it with you, tempting them with the prospect of free access to your huge stock of Atari video games or a chance to scatter your specially procured soiled paper hand towels all over the bathroom.

CHEZ WALLY

Being a Wally doesn't end when you come home in the evening, shut the front door behind you and slump down in front of the telly. It's an all-embracing life-style – and that means that your home should be Wally too. Imagine how shaming it would be, for instance, to invite a few of your Wally friends back to your home for a mug of banana Nesquick and a Rich Tea biscuit after a night at the pub, and have to usher them into a house full of stripped pine and glass-mounted National Theatre posters! Spare yourself a few blushes and muttered apologies by making sure that your home unambiguously reflects your status as a Wally. Follow the advice in this section and you won't put a foot wrong.

Wally-Plan

When it comes to furnishing your home, there's no room for half measures. Avoid at all costs the type of decorative and aesthetic gaffes so many novice Wallies are prone to: the careless juxtaposition of a Habitat table lamp with a set of walnut veneer nesting tables from John Lewis; the ghastly blunder of scattering poncy floral cushions from Laura Ashley all over your Times Furnishing settee. Lesson Number One is: have the courage of your convictions. Be a Wally – and let your surroundings prove you're one.

Take the lounge, for example. *Don't* waste time, energy and money commissioning a firm of interior decorators to create for you a dynamic split-level living environment consisting of acres of white wool carpet and tubular steel furniture with the pipe work and electricity cables daringly exposed. Don't muck it up by going for shrill primary colours, natural wood or Abyssinian wall-hangings. All you want in your lounge is space in which to put up your Steve Davis Fold-Away Mini-Snooker table and congenial surroundings in which to bash out a tune a day on the home organ, kick the cat, bolt down a TV dinner, mix yourself a drink at the bar and possibly ask a few friends round for a screening of your Task Force Special tapes on the video. You require, in short, a room in which you can open a Watney's Party Four without fear of causing irreparable damage to a priceless Henry Moore lithograph – and you definitely want those pipes and cables out of sight so that you can whack a nail through them when you come to hang a picture.

Textiles. In Wally homes, practical and aesthetic considerations should go hand in hand. Carpets, for example, should be of man-made fibre in swirling multi-coloured designs so that fag ends, crisps, half-eaten Jammie Dodgers and anything else that doesn't get gobbled up by the Alsatian can be trodden in without leaving a trace. Sofas and chairs should be upholstered in wipe-clean leatherette for similar sound practical reasons. And wall surfaces should be heavily textured, either with flock wallpapers, anaglyptas or Sandtex Fine Build, so that when the odd plateful of Vesta Beef Curry or take-away Chinese goes flying across the room and gets stuck to the wall it can pass more or less unnoticed.

Patterns and colour schemes. Your only purely aesthetic foible should concern stripes. Bold stripes in bright colours belong on cars, toothpaste and down the sleeves of anoraks – not on walls. Beyond that, you should refuse to be fettered by conventional notions about clashing patterns or the inadvisability of combining chintz with tartan and polka dots. If you hit on a combination that makes your eyes water and evokes either Carnival Week in Rio or Mardi Gras in New Orleans, you'll know you're on the right lines.

Colour can be a problem area for the Wally home furnisher, mainly because your ideas are liable to be heavily conditioned by the kind of milk-and-water schemes you've seen in magazines like *Homes and Gardens*, where the major aim is to provide a muted background for those rows and rows of unread Penguins with their vivid orange spines. Your first step in choosing a colour scheme is to clear your mind of these pernicious influences. Remember: Wallies do not make 'statements' in gentle pastel shades, nor do they use cunning colour contrasts in order to create a feeling of space or to bring the walls in closer or the ceiling down lower. If you want to lower a ceiling, the way to do it is to puncture a waterbed or leave the taps running on the floor above.

Further, the kind of statements you want to make in your home cannot be made with conventional colours such as Magnolia, Honeysuckle, Oyster or Dusky Pink; they have to be made with the following range of Wally-Plan Specials:

- Sour Cream
- Rosy Nipple
- Thames Mud
- Snot green
- Branston Pickle
- Scarlet Fever
- Caramel Custard
- Channel Grey
- Cow Pat
- Hot Flush
- Danish Blue
- Piccallilli
- Bladderwrack
- Curious Yellow
- Tabasco
- Mushy Pea

Also, if you *have* to choose one of those subtle 'White? Not Quite' shades, make it one of the following: Slightly Soiled, Deathly Pale, or Top of the Milk.

Furniture. No hard and fast rules here. Go for robustness and durability obviously, but not at the expense of unsightliness. Don't be fooled into buying supposedly 'period' furniture which has been artificially aged in a repro workshop. If anyone's going to put ring marks, scratches, dents, chips and inkstains all over your furniture, it should be you.

Ornaments and decorative items. The key word here is 'overkill'. Don't make the mistake of decorating your G-Plan sideboard with a single tasteful spray of 'Soft Silk' washable fabric flowers and expect to score points for showing classic restraint and decorum. Your miserliness with the knick-knacks will simply allow your friends to indulge the suspicion that you're not fully conversant with the range of Wally ornaments and that the washable flowers were a fluke. They could even draw the conclusion that you didn't choose them yourself at all, but had them given to you by a friend and that secretly you hate the sight of them.

To be absolutely sure of creating the right impression, fill every corner of your home with all of the following:

- Framed colour prints of Alpine scenes
- Caithness glass paperweights
- Shakespearian 'character' jugs
- Handpainted stoneware rabbits, unicorns and field birds
- Royal Doulton 'Bunnykins' figurines
- Decorative herb sachets in the form of owls, cats, etc.
- Wax candles in the form of fruit and vegetables
- Miniature bone china wheelbarrows full of flowers
- Raffia-bound Chianti bottles or leather Sangria decanters
- Porcelain figures of Victorian Nannies, Old Sea Dogs, Pirates, Mr Pickwick, Huckleberry Finn and Winston Churchill
- Crocheted lavatory-roll holders in the form of poodles
- Flamenco dolls
- Tretchikoff and David Shepherd prints
- Photographs of yourself in Victorian or Wild West costume
- Glass bells and engraved Regency brandy-snifters
- Bullfight posters with your name printed in place of the matador's
- Ivory and bronze figures of Ian Botham, Dennis Lillee etc. in the 'Arlott's Immortals' series
- Shimmering fibre-optic whatsits
- Cylindrical illuminated thingummies

(See also *How to buy a sumptuous hand-crafted Objet d'Art*, p. 60)

When it comes to the actual fabric of your home, you could be lucky and find yourself living in a house that already has ill-fitting doors, paper-thin walls, 4-inch soil pipes running through the lounge and light switches put on at peculiar angles. On the other hand, you could find that you have to add these essential features yourself, by slaving away with a Black and Decker in your spare evenings and at weekends. Usually, though, even if your house *was* either jerrybuilt originally or extensively botched up by a previous owner, you will still wish to add some little touches of your own, simply to imprint your personality on it. You could be ambitious and transform the exterior in the manner shown in the diagramon p. 91. Or you could just add features such as a home sauna, a bar in the lounge, Wild West saloon doors, a handsome brick fireplace surround or simply a little porcelain sign on the loo door saying '*Yer Tiz*'.

The only proper way to go about these tasks is to Do Them Yourself. As a Wally, you should in any case be a DIY fanatic, for the following reasons:

1) DIY is manly and nous-intensive and gives you an excuse to wear grubby overalls, carry a steel tape measure in your pocket, stick ciggies and stubs of pencil behind your ear, and for once in your life look as if you know what you're doing.
2) DIY affords endless opportunities to fall off ladders, get splinters in your bottom, slice the top off your fingers, get your head stuck in buckets and electrocute yourself – all under the pretext of doing useful jobs about the house.
3) DIY enables you not only to embellish your own home with louvre doors and polystyrene ceiling tiles from MFI, but also, when visiting friends' houses, to go around pointing out cracks in the plaster and patches of dry rot and woodworm, prodding the walls with your pocket Dampometer, tut-tutting, shaking your head gloomily, whistling through your teeth and generally volunteering vast amounts of unwanted advice.

Wally DIY should not be confused with conventional DIY. Conventional DIY is easy. All you have to do is make sure you've got the right tools to hand, estimate materials sensibly and set about each job methodically. Wally DIY is hard – and it's still hard even when you know how. To begin with, it calls for a number of skills which you're *not* going to pick up from the Reader's Digest *Book of the Home*: the skill of guiding a power-saw while simultaneously hand-rolling a cigarette and reading your horoscope in the *Daily Mirror*; wiring up an extra spur on the ring main with the power on; wriggling your way under the floorboards while holding a lighted match in order to check for gas leaks; that special knack of demolishing load-bearing walls without being crushed to death by an avalanche of falling masonry. There are some jobs, frankly, that turn out to be beyond the scope of even the most enthusiastic Wally DIY-er; in such cases, all you can do is swallow your pride and call in a firm of cowboys to do the job for you.

Building an extension to your home. This can not only greatly enlarge your living space and add a whole new dimension to your home, it can also be a very useful way of using up all the polystyrene ceiling tiles and louvre doors you over-ordered on your last DIY project. An extension with a flat felt roof covered with gravel chippings also makes an excellent outdoor cat litter.

The conventional way to go about building an extension is to start with the foundations and work your way upwards, leaving the roof till last. This isn't by any means the only method, but it does at least have the virtue of allowing you to tackle the most enjoyable bit first. This is where you recreate a First World War battle-scene in your back garden by stripping to the waist, marching out into the pouring rain, digging down through four feet of solid clay, putting a pickaxe through the mains drainage channel and catching either pneumonia or Trench Foot. The other advantage is that should you discover at this early stage that your garden has a high water table, *i.e.* floods of water lying inches below the surface, there's still time to abandon

Wally Home Improvement

Before ...

After …

your scheme for an extension and think about a swimming pool instead.

Work in progress. Whatever project you decide on, whether it's a pool, a granny annexe for the wife and kids or a multi-level sun patio consisting of acres of pink and yellow crazy paving, perforated concrete balustrades, plastic birdbaths and floodlit fountains, don't forget to keep a complete step-by-step photographic record of the building work with which to bore the pants off your friends at social gatherings. This should be in the form of an imitation leather photo album containing pictures of you (1) ceremonially cutting the first sod or taking the first wild swing with a sledgehammer; (2) giving a cheerful thumbs-up to the camera, blissfully unaware that the concrete lintel above your head is about to give away, burying you under a couple of tons of breeze-blocks; (3) grinning ruefully as you attempt to extract your wellies from six inches of quick-setting ready-mix concrete; (4) reversing a hired mechanical digger into your next-door neighbour's garden fence; and finally (5) proudly glueing the last strip of woodgrain laminate or polystyrene ceiling tile in position while perched precariously on the top of a step ladder.

With each project you tackle, your collection of photo albums should grow, until eventually they take up so much room in your home that you have to build a special photo album extension to accomodate them. You will then be able to record the building of the photo album extension in an especially lavish photo album extension album.

Painting and decorating. Wall-papering and painting are well within the scope of the Wally DIY enthusiast, and it requires surprisingly little effort to make a really spectacular pig's dinner of both. In fact, hanging a strip of wall-paper crooked or upside down, or so that the pattern doesn't match up is *so* easy that in order to do it you don't really have to be a Wally at all – which is bound to take away somewhat from the satisfaction you'll feel with the end result.

Painting, too, is made almost *too* easy for you by the fact that so often the paint inside the tin bears no relation at all to the colour on the lid or chart. It's therefore as easy to hit on a Wally colour scheme by accident as to sit down for hours with a set of colour charts and really work at it.

Take care to prepare all surfaces properly before you start painting. There are several proprietary paint strippers on the market that do an excellent job of removing layers of human skin but few that work as well on layers of old paint. If you have a large area of old paint you want stripped, eat a garlic mayonnaise burger and six packets of cheese and onion crisps and try breathing on it.

Energy-saving in the home. Never waste money by allowing precious heat to escape through your roof or through draughty windows or doors. Instead, waste money by installing costly and ineffective double-glazing.

WALLIES SANS FRONTIERES

The Wally Holiday Guide

The holiday season begins early these days. To be exact, it begins as you sit in a post-Christmas daze, gazing blankly at the second commercial break in the annual Boxing Day screening of The Sound of Music (the first commercial break having been entirely given over to ads announcing fabulous reductions and sale bargains at Debenham's). Dimly you perceive through a swirling haze of Henri Winterman smoke and Creme de Menthe fumes that the bikini-clad girl waving at you from a speedboat in Torremolinos is altogether too generously endowed to be Julie Andrews. Then realisation dawns. What you're watching isn't The Sound of Music at all. It's the first holiday ad of the year – which means that the time has come once more to think about booking up for your annual dose of instant sunburn and foreign tummy ...

Being a Wally holidaymaker used to be easy. All you had to do was go on a package holiday to Benidorm and spend a fortnight cheek by jowl with hordes of pleasure-seekers from Birmingham and Wolverhampton, stuffing your face with paiella and chips and manfully lending a hand with the building work on your hotel. Nowadays it's not so simple. The problem is, there just aren't enough half-finished Spanish holiday hotels to go round any more. Another problem is that a hundred and one equally enticing Wally-traps also beckon, every one of them bristling with Kojak bars, Travolta discos, British pubs serving fizzy keg beers and nightclubs offering superb evening entertainment by top European Cabaret Artistes.

So where do you go these days if you want Delhi Belly but you don't want to go to India for it?

The answer is that you don't have to go anywhere. A perfectly acceptable Wally holiday is simply to steam aimlessly back and forth across the English Channel, drinking yourself blind on duty-free booze and falling down the companionways. You could also take the advice contained in the Wally caravanning guide and stick to the British Isles, enjoying some of the splendid hold-ups and tailbacks listen on pp. 104-6. But if you are intent on going abroad and giving the locals a free course of instruction in how to be a Wally and you don't know which resort to choose, there's one rule of thumb you can always apply. Instead of wasting hours poring over travel brochures, simply ask yourself, Is it the kind of place where Bobby Moore might open a nightclub? If the answer's yes, it's safe to go ahead and book up. But *hurry*.

Planning your Wally package holiday

The success of your Wally package holiday depends to a great extent on luck. There are always the thousand-to-one-against disasters that no amount of careful planning can forestall: for instance, you might be travelling economy class to Tenerife and find yourself engaged in conversation by an international lawyer or surrounded by a party of nuns. You could book a holiday in Malta and find when you got there that by some extraordinary freak you'd hit on the one time of year when there wasn't another English tourist in sight. You could just be cracking a tube of lager on the back seat of your Cosmos Tourama coach when you discover that by some administrative blunder you've been assigned to a tour that involves being rudely dragged out of the coach at intervals and forced to footslog it round art galleries, museums and ancient monuments ...

Equally, there are always the unexpected bonuses. You might for instance time your holiday to coincide with a baggagehandlers' strike or a work to rule by port officials, and end up spending an unforgettable week camping in an airport departure lounge or sunning yourself on the quayside at Dover. It's swings and roundabouts all the way with holidays.

However, between the two extremes of the unexpected boons and the unexpected disasters, there's a vast amount that you can achieve by planning. Do your best to ensure that your Wally Continental package includes at least one of the following essential ingredients.

Overbooking. Remember the famous state-room scene in the Marx Brothers' A Night At The Opera? Aim for the same scenes of mayhem and confusion on board your plane or ship or on arrival at your holiday hotel or villa. Method: place all booking arrangements in the hands of one of the less reputable tour operators and they'll take care of everything.

A six-hour wait at Luton airport. Is it possible to get *anywhere* from Luton airport? Find out the hard way. Guaranteed to get your holiday off to a flying start eventually.

Lost luggage. You spend two weeks in Lido di Jesolo in the clothes you stand up in. Your luggage has the holiday of a lifetime in Honolulu. Simple to arrange: some airlines do it as a matter of course.

Sunburn. The Lobster Look renders you immediately recognisable as a Wally and avoids any risk of you being mistaken for a run-of-the-mill holidaymaker. Method: one way is to motor down to the Algarve in one hop, strip off on arrival and flop down in an exhausted heap in a fierce sun for a few hours. Practise by falling asleep under your sun-ray lamp.

Holiday tummy. Comes in two forms. There's no need to miss out by only going down with one of them; simply exceed the stated Senakot dose and you'll have a full house.

Useful Phrases for Continental Holidays

Out and about

Can you direct me to the nearest bar serving lukewarm Barbican?
Pouvez-vous me diriger au bar le plus proche servant de la Barbican tiède?
Pueded dirigirme al bar más cercano dénde sirven Barbican templado?
My pedal boat has been struck by a freak tidal wave.
Mon pedale-bateau été frappé par une vague de fond capricieuse.
Un maremoto extraordinario ha volcado mi patin.
This square foot of beach is already taken.
Ce pied carré de la plage a été pris déjà.
Este metro quadrado de playa ya está ocupado.
The fat German from Room 903 has just spontaneously combusted by the poolside.
Le gros allemand dans la chambre numero 903 a spontanément combusté au bord de la piscine.
El alemán gordo de la habitacion 903 hacaba de estallar en llamas espontaniamente al lado de la piscina.

At the police

My St Christopher medallion became entangled with this young lady's belt buckle at a Club Wally beach barbecue.
Mon medaillon St Christophe s'est entanglé avec la ceinture de cette jeune fille au barbecue du Club Wally.
Mi medalla de S. Cristóbal se enredo con la hebilla de su cinturón en la barbacoa playera del Club Wally.
I only wanted one as a souvenir.
Je le voulais seulement comme souvenir.
Solo queria uno como recuerdo.

In the restuarant

I have got my head stuck in an ice bucket.
J'ai coincé ma tête dans le seau à glaçons.
Tengo mi cabeza atascada en un cubo de hielo.

I seem to have left my American Express card in the Cortina.
Il semble que j'ai oublié ma carte American Express dans la Cortina.
Me parece que me he dejado mi tarjeta del American Express en el Cortina.
When I want Ambre Solaire on my salad, I'll ask for it, thank you.
Quand j'aurai besoin d'une vinaigrette à l'Ambre Solaire, je vous la demanderai, merci.
Cuando quiera Ambre Solaire en mi ensalata, se lo pediré, gracias.

At the disco

Come outside and say that.
Venez dehors et répétez cela.
Sal a fuera a decirmelo.

At the doctor's

And the next thing I knew, he stuck one on me.
Et tout à coup, il m'en a collé un.
A continuación, lo que pasó es que me pegó una.
I have scorched my upper lip on a glass of flaming Sambucca.
J'ai brûlé ma lèvre supérieure avec un verre de Sambucca flambant.
Me he quemado el labio superior con un vaso de Zambucca quemante.
I have been struck on the epiglotis by a frisbee.
Mon épiglotte a été heurtée par un frisbi.
Me han dado en la epiglotis con un frisbee.
My friend has a pink cocktail parasol lodged in his windpipe.
Mon ami a un parasole rose de cocktail coincé dans son gosier.
Mi amigo tiene un parasolillo de coctel de color rosa atascado en la trachea.

At the boutique

I'll take the one with the Go Faster stripes.
Je prends celle avec les rayures de vitesse.
Me quedo el que tiene las correas de velocidad.

At the customs

I swear to God I've never seen them before in my life.
Je jure devant Dieu, Monsieur l'inspecteur douanier, que je ne les ai jamais vu de ma vie.
Se lo juro por Dios que no las he visto en mi vida.

The Wally Guide to Holiday Activities on the Continent

Simply by choosing to take a holiday in a place like Marbella or Ostend you will already have given evidence to suggest that you are a Wally. But of course it doesn't end there.

While abroad, it is your duty to demonstrate your skills to the local residents and to prove to them that when it comes to being a Wally, the British can still teach the world a thing or two. You can do this in a number of ways, ranging from simply failing to observe the most elementary hygeine and safety precautions to performing acts of bravado or daring abandon such as leaping on to the table in a Spanish nightclub with a rose clenched between your teeth and flamenco-dancing in your underpants or conducting mock bull-fights using tablecloths and a sweet trolley. More suggestions are given below.

Being a Wally on the Continent means hard work and long hours, often for very little reward other than the occasional volley of derision from other holidaymakers and the water-cannon, CS gas or rubber truncheon treatment from local police or paramilitaries. But don't be too downcast if you have to spend a few days picking cockroaches out of your soup in a sweltering lockup somewhere on the Costa del Sol. Remember: if enough other Wallies follow your example, the message will eventually get through to your host nation. And think of the satisfaction you'll feel when hordes of Spanish Wallies come pouring off the ferry at Southampton, wearing plastic Union Jack bowlers and blowing whoopee whistles, and set about laying waste to the south of England.

Defacing or chipping pieces off ancient monuments. If you are ever unfortunate enough to find yourself whisked off against your will and forced to gawp admiringly at ancient relics, one way to make the experience just about bearable is to carve your initials all over the monuments in question or break off a chunk to take home to show your friends. Try to get in a bit of practice before you go abroad by spraying Wallies Rule OK all over Stonehenge with a blue aerosol. The famous figure of Winged Victory in the Louvre with both arms missing shows what you can achieve if you put your mind to it.

Causing an affray in nightclubs and discos. Don't leave it all to the professional footballers and the sailors on shore leave. Build up gradually to a fully-fledged brawl by persistently shouting for the band to play 'Una Paloma Blanca', 'Viva Espana' or 'The Birdy Song' and chanting or slow-handclapping through the cabaret. Then needle the locals by taking to the stage yourself, drink in hand, singing a chorus of 'Roll Out The Barrel', making jocular reference to the Spanish Armada, the bloody nose we Brits gave the French at Agincourt, the Italian book of War Heroes, or touching on some other obvious sore spot or raw nerve. Round off your performance by drinking a toast to Margaret Thatcher and death to all Argies, and – assuming you're still in one piece – step down and join in the bunfight which by now should be well under way on the night-club floor.

Hotel or football stadium demolition. A vital activity, not to be left for those rare occasions when you can pop across the Channel for a football international or for your even rarer World Cup all-in-one package holiday, but ideally an integral part of every Continental excursion. There's nothing that Hitler could do with a couple of Panzer Divisions that you and the lads can't tackle comfortably with your bare hands – so get out there and prove it.

Making an exhibition of yourself on waterskis. Everybody does this when they're learning, but in your case it's different: you go on falling in time after time after time and never get any better at it. This should be enough to convince spectators on the beach that you're a Wally, but if not, try waterskiing while fully clothed, wearing a silly hat or while drinking from a can of Tuborg.

Shopping for souvenirs. Buying trinkets and mementos on the Continent is easy in the sense that in many foreign resorts there's very little else you can buy, but tricky in that it often requires large amounts of money and gullibility. When buying a picture of a little Neapolitan boy with a tear rolling down his cheek or a souvenir-of-Brussels corkscrew you sometimes find yourself being asked to believe that they're the work of local craftsmen – and to pay accordingly.

Caravanning

If you want to spend a Wally fortnight in the British Isles, you couldn't do better than to take a caravan holiday.

One of the great attractions of caravanning is the freedom it gives you. With a 'van' snaking around dangerously behind your car and the open road ahead of you, you're no longer tied down to busy resorts where thousands sit packed like sardines and the stretcher parties can hardly fight their way through the crowds to remove the sunstroke victims. You can go where you like, free as a bird – *and yet still be a Wally.*

This is because caravanning imposes on you an intrinsically Wally life-style, whether you're in splendid isolation in the Peak District or surrounded by endless rows of mobile homes overlooking a gravel pit somewhere in the Thames Valley.

When caravanning, you *have* to eat off Melamine picnic ware and park your bottom on gaily decorated tubular aluminium picnic chairs; you *have* to venture into dark and smelly campsite washrooms, having first made an epic journey past miles of other caravans full of jeering holidaymakers while nervously clutching a torch, a roll of

Andrex and a plastic sponge bag. You *have* to hang Airwicks everywhere to dispel that lingering aroma of fried sausage and Elsan, and drink lukewarm ready-mixed gin and tonic or whisky and ginger ale from screw-top bottles You have to do these things because there is no other way to do them when living in a caravan. Just as there is no such thing as a conservatively dressed limbo dancer or an Indian restaurant with no red-flock wallpaper, so there is no such thing as a non-Wally caravan. You are halfway to being a Wally the moment you step inside one.

But *only* halfway. In order to go the full distance, you must bear in mind the following points:

1) The optimum size for a Wally caravan is always 'too small'. So if you buy one that's not much bigger than a tin of Old Holborn to begin with, you start with an advantage. If on the other hand you go for one of the more opulent and spacious models, it's vital to give it that 'no room to swing a cat' feeling by cluttering it up with colour televisions, ghetto blasters, microwave ovens, and sandwich toasters, even possibly by aralditing a few ornamental knick-knacks in position in or around the window ledges.
2) All genuinely Wally caravans have frilly net curtains or dress drapes in the windows.
3) All genuinely Wally caravans are pitched in the corner of the field or campsite reserved exclusively for Wallies. *I.e.*, the one where other campers or caravanners are in the habit of emptying their tea-leaves, orange peel and slops.
4) All genuinely Wally caravanners belong to the Caravan Club – but not all Caravan Club members are Wallies. However, you do *have* to be a Wally in order to thrill to the prospect of spending a weekend with total strangers on a caravan site somewhere on the outskirts of Birmingham discussing towbars, awnings and the latest developments in the technology of the chemical toilet.

In order to be a genuine Wally caravanner you must not

make the mistake of looking on your caravanning holiday as an opportunity for rest and relaxation in peaceful surroundings. It is nothing of the sort. Essentially, it is a chance to practise being a Wally householder, only in more cramped, uncomfortable and therefore challenging conditions. Your morning routine should be gruelling: getting dressed, converting the sleeping area to the eating area by folding away the bedding and erecting the stow-away table, eating breakfast, washing up, shaking out the rugs and cushions, fetching water and emptying the you-know-whats and returning all the cutlery and cooking utensils to their proper place in cunningly concealed drawers and hidden cupboards ...

If you follow roughly the same procedure in the afternoon and evening, you should find that you're left with virtually no time at all in which to relax and enjoy yourself, but if you do find you have a spare moment, the correct thing to do is to remove yourself from the scene altogether by lifting up one of the seats, climbing into the coffin-like recess below, closing the lid down on top of you and staying there in a Dracula pose with your hands across your chest until it's time to get out and prepare the next meal.

WHERE TO FIND THOSE HOLIDAY TRAFFIC JAMS

For holiday-makers in the British Isles, finding those queues of holiday traffic used to be a hit-and-miss affair. Sometimes you could strike lucky and find yourself slap-bang in the middle of a ten-mile tailback, other times it was plain sailing all the way and you just had to be content with causing a traffic jam of your own. Now, thanks to this easy-to-follow guide, you can plan your route so as to take in the very best of Britain's traffic trouble spots and 'pinch points'.

Key

Danger. Egon Ronay-recommended gastronomic black spot.

Tailback Zone

Motorway

A Road

B Road

1 Thanks to a sudden shortage of motorway where the M6 fizzles out at Carlisle you have to crawl along at a snail's pace all the way to the ferry at Stranraer and probably miss your boat. Ideal for the family Wally.

2 The A65 between Leeds and the M6 – notorious.

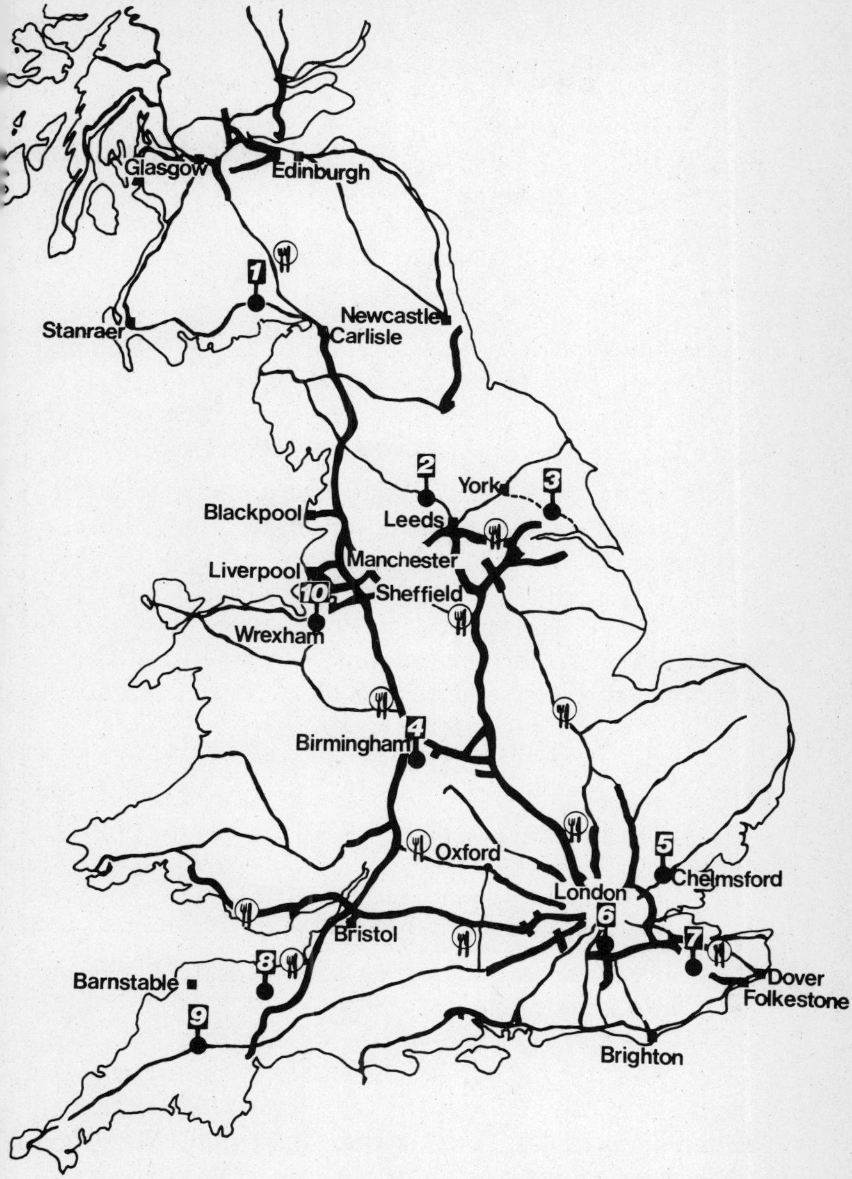
Glasgow
Edinburgh
1
Stanraer
Newcastle
Carlisle
2
York
3
Blackpool
Leeds
Liverpool
Manchester
10
Sheffield
Wrexham
4
Birmingham
5
Oxford
Chelmsford
London
6
Bristol
7
8
Barnstable
Dover
Folkestone
9
Brighton

3

The A1079 between the Humber Road Bridge and York is worth a visit. Market Weighton will be by-passed in 1986 so enjoy the delays while you can.

4

A missing motorway link between the M5 and M42 south-east of Birmingham creates all-the-year-round carve-ups.

5

X-certificate hold-ups at Chelmsford as you steam out of London bound for the East Coast holiday resorts.

6

Picturesque scenes as holiday and commercial traffic from Brighton and Newhaven disgorges into Coulsdon and Purley.

7

A classic bottleneck as motorway traffic from Dover and Folkestone converges on the old A20 trunk road.

8

For mile-long queues in beautiful surroundings, try this popular stretch of the A361 from the M5 to Barnstaple.

9

Explore grockle country on the superbly congested A30 via Okehampton.

10

The spectacular A483 from Chester to Wrexham makes an ideal holiday route to North Wales for orange-peel and sandwich droppers from Liverpool and Manchester.

HOW TO BE A WALLY AT WORK

Some people are lucky. They have jobs that specifically require them to be Wallies. Door to door double-glazing salesmen, for example. Secondhand car dealers. Local radio disc jockeys. The Lionel Blair Dancers. The Game For A Laugh team. People who sell battery-operated yipping dogs on the pavement in Oxford Street or appear in commercials for Barratt's Homes.

Others are lucky too. Though not contractually bound to be Wallies, they at least have jobs that enable them to dress up in funny clothes and go around looking like Wallies: traffic wardens; Mormons; Butlin's Redcoats; or people who shovel chips into paper bags at Macdonalds or Kentuckies.

But the vast majority are less fortunate. For them, work offers very little opportunity either to behave like a Wally or even to look like one. They have to content themselves with being weekend or spare-time Wallies – or else somehow try and do a job and be a Wally simultaneously.

In practice, combining both is extremely difficult. The problem is, of course, that being a Wally is more than just arduous and time-consuming – *it's a full-time job in itself* (see Job Description, pp. 108-9).

If you doubt this, consider the plight of Wally Post Office clerks. Many of them are so busy being Wallies that they can barely spare the time to issue stamps and television licences. Or take the case of the hard-pressed Wallies who deal with Passenger Enquiries for British Rail. Usually they're so rushed off their feet being Wallies that it takes them a good five minutes before they can get round to answering the phone – and very often they are still busy being Wallies when they do.

As a beginner, your first step towards becoming a Wally at work is to be realistic about what you can and can't achieve. Don't be too ambitious at the outset. In fact, don't be ambitious at all. You'll have quite enough on your plate

Job Description

Position: Full-time Resident Wally (ungraded)

1. Position of job

To liaise with other Wallies within the office or department and externally regarding the previous evening's telly, the prospect of Millwall being relegated to the Fourth Division the lamentable decline in the quality of the chips in the staff canteen, and to adjudicate in such matters as which female member of staff sports the largest pair of knockers. To organise the procurement of giant-size birthday cards for other members of staff and to inscribe them with obscene limericks or snatches of self-penned doggerel. To score own goals for the office football team and sit on ground for minutes afterwards holding head in hands. To slag off and badmouth superiors. To conduct campaigns of sexual harassment against secretaries and receptionists. To sunbathe in the office car park. To ensure that the air is at all times heavily laden with the rich aroma of sweaty armpits, nylon or polyester shirts, bad breath and Player's No. 6. To be last out of the building during fire drills. To generally promote the spread of the British Disease.

2. Position within organisation

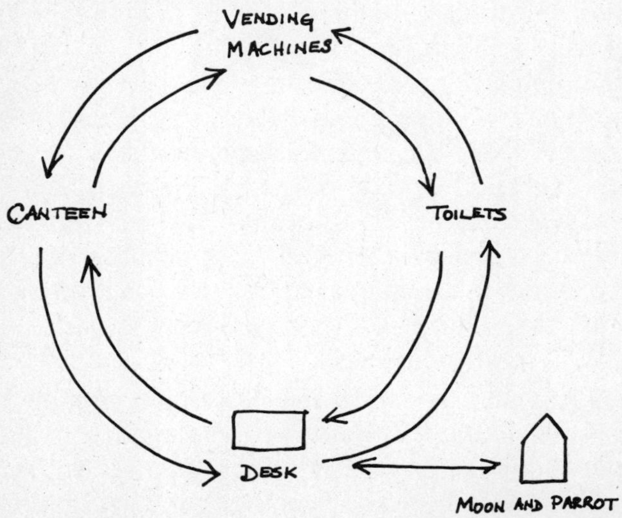

3. <u>Functional relationships/contacts</u>

Internal

Members of the office squash league, darts team, or magazine circle.
Other Dolly Parton fans.
Other Capri drivers
People selling LPs, Videos, or cut-price tickets for Evita via staff noticeboard.

External

The Speaking Clock
Dial A Disc
Cricketline
Total strangers who phone up out of the blue for confidential chats about personal finance

4. Additional duties

a) Perform strip-tease on top of filing cabinet during office Christmas party.
b) Get accidentally separated from rest of party during Staff Association coach trip to Munich beer festival.
c) Provide light show and disco for annual company dinner.
d) Go on the rampage during sales conferences, setting off fire extinguishers and destroying hotel furniture.
e) Conduct interesting culinary experiments in the canteen by heaping all the leftovers onto one plate, adding custard and salad cream and stirring to a thick paste.
f) Perpetrate vile smells in the toilets.
g) To be permanently sozzled during exhibitions and trade fairs and wear lapel badge upside down.

Meetings attended

Informal think-tank cum creative barnstorming session in saloon bar of Moon and Parrot (most lunchtimes).
Occassional Gin Rummy school in Post Room on Friday afternoons.

Job holder's Approval A.Wally

simply trying to combine being a Wally and being an office junior. Being a Wally and a Captain of Industry comes later. Certainly it calls for skills beyond the scope of a book like this.

The Wally Desk Kit

You cannot hope to discharge your duties as a Wally efficiently unless you have all the necessary equipment to hand. If you work in an office, this means staking out your own little corner of the corporate battlefield and littering it with the following essential aids to executive time-wasting:

1) Notices saying
   Quick! Look Busy. Here comes the Boss!
   The impossible we can do today. Miracles take a little longer.
   You don't have to be mad to work here – but it helps!
   As soon as I can spare the time I'm going to have a nervous breakdown. I've worked for it. I deserve it. No one's going to stop me!
   Why is there always so much month left at the end of the money?
   Wake up with a smile on your face. Sleep with a coathanger in your mouth.
   The world is full of willing people. Some willing to work. Others willing to let them.
   A clean desk is the sign of a sick mind.
   Tomorrow we are going to get organised.
   Laurel and Hardy could do it better!
   Keep smiling – the boss loves idiots.
2) Postcards, preferably dirty ones, from approved Wally holiday resorts.
3) Mascots, rosettes, cuddly toys, team photos and travel posters.
4) Novelty biros, a plastic zip-up pencil case in the form of a giant pencil, a giant plastic comb, a Snoopy pencil sharpener.

5) At least one plastic or paper cup from the office vending machine containing half an inch of cold tea or coffee with a fag-end floating in it.
6) A perspex photo cube containing risque snaps of your uproarious Club Wally holiday in Aghios Nikolaos or Mykonos.
7) An impenetrable sight-screen consisting of rubber plants, Busy Lizzies, maidenhair ferns and castor oil plants, all with fags stubbed out around the base, and liberally watered with vending-machine Bovril.
8) And in the drawers of your desk: squash balls, your very own ping pong bat, a sweatband, Baby Bio, Muscleman Protein Plus Tablets, and huge volumes of awkward correspondence, memos you're sitting on until you can find a way of quietly disposing of them or smuggling them out of the office without anybody noticing.

Planning your day

One of the many frustrating experiences you'll encounter as a Wally in the office is to be sitting quietly at your desk among the fluffy toys and novelties, putting the finishing touches to your prototype for a vertical take-off paper dart, when to your intense annoyance you're suddenly disturbed by a telephone call on some trifling matter from a customer, supplier or member of the public, or by an urgent request from your boss to drop everything and get on to so-and-so in the Accounts department, file an important batch of paperclips, or, more usually, to investigate the non-appearance of his 40 Capstan Full Strengths and mid-morning bacon roll. Given your crowded schedule, this is exactly the kind of distraction you could do without. But how do you avoid it?

You can't, unfortunately. But you can minimise the inconvenience.

One solution is to try to plan ahead, sorting your various tasks into a properly graded list of priorities, so that when the unexpected crisis does crop up and you have no alternative but to get your finger out, you can still plan around it and salvage something from the day. For example, perhaps on this particular occasion you could cut short your usual three-hour stint propping up the bar at the Moon and Parrot at lunchtime and finish the paper dart then. Or you could shelve the project for the meantime and instead try making a Mickey Mouse out of Blue-Tac or removing the crust on your Tippex, or turn your attention to something less labour-intensive, such as nobbling the office vending machine or simply walking up and down on the nylon floor carpet giving people electric shocks.

Of course, it's not always possible to do this. You can't do everything. There are, after all, only so many hours in the day and you have even fewer than most because as a Wally you work to a personal Flexitime scheme which involves being last into the office in the morning and first out at knocking off time. Sometimes you simply have to explain to people that they'll have to wait and that you're fully occupied filling in a questionnaire in *Penthouse* to find out your sexual I.Q. Not in so many words, of course, but by using one of the following time-honoured phrases:

'More than my job's worth ...'
'Not my pigeon ...'
'Up to my eyeballs ...'
'Just a cog in a wheel ...'
'Only one pair of hands ...'

Alternatively, you can send them a letter or memo thanking them for bringing the matter to your notice and assuring them that it is now receiving your most urgent attention.

How to be an executive Wally

No matter how hard you try and avoid it, if you work in any kind of organisation the chances are that sooner or later you're going to get promoted. Usually this is through no fault of your own – just a case of poor judgement on the part of superiors or dead men's shoes.

Often your promotion comes just at a time when you're beginning to get the hang of being a Wally office junior – and it's an undeniable blow. But there are compensations. For a start, life on the lower rungs of the management ladder doesn't necessarily mean more work and less time to be a Wally – often quite the opposite. Secondly, although it does require you to clean up your act somewhat, the changes are cosmetic rather than functional.

Being an executive Wally means no more Male Chauvinist Pig ties and polyester shirts with racing cars dotted all over them. Instead you sport blue stripey shirts with white collars and snazzy three-piece suits from Harry Fenton with jackets that you hang from a little hook behind the driving seat of your company car. Your entire personal appearance becomes smarter, better-groomed. You affect huge gold sovereign ring mounts and a Kevin Keegan hairdo which you pat and preen constantly and check nervously in shop windows; you carry a slim attaché case containing top-secret Kleenex tissues and confidential battery shaver. You no longer pinch bottoms or sneak glances up secretaries' skirts on the stairs; instead you wine and dine them at alcove tables in Italian restaurants and restrict yourself to a furtive grope over the Zabaglione. You no longer pollute the entire department with No. 6 smoke; you've switched to Silk Cut with the odd Slim Panatella – and anyway, you now have an office of your own where you can cough and splutter to your heart's content. As an executive Wally you are more fastidious in matters of personal hygeine too. Where you once emitted ray-gun bursts of raw onion after ploughman's lunches at the Moon and Parrot, you now exude the faintest tang of expense-account garlic mushroom laced with Tic Tac, Polo Mint or Gold Spot. And you no longer smell of armpits and Brut, you smell of Hai-Karate.

As an executive Wally your desk kit, too, is restrained by comparison with your Wally underlings. No profusion of placards, football colours or travel posters here; instead, just a Newton's Cradle, a photo of the wife and kids, and – to show that underneath it all nothing has *really* changed – a plummeting sales graph.

HOW TO BE A SUPERWALLY

What is a Superwally?

A Superwally is someone who drives a Porsche with a sticker in the rear window that says 'My Other Car's A Porsche'. He has mirror-glass installed in his office the wrong way round. He builds a Californian conversation pit in his ranch-style residence in Surrey even though he has nothing to converse about.

A Superwally is someone who keeps a gold-plated personalised pocket calculator cum alarm clock in the breast pocket of his monogrammed silk pyjamas so that he can be woken up in the mornings by an electronic version of the James Bond theme.

Above all, a Superwally is someone whose idea of travelling incognito consists of riding around in a Rolls Royce Silver Cloud with personalised numberplate flanked by motorcycle outriders and police escort – but with his dark glasses on.

How do you become a Superwally? Frankly, your chances are almost nil. You certainly won't do it by hard work, or by taking a correspondence course in business studies, or by following the kind of advice that can be given in a book such as this. You can only become a Superwally by a unique combination of 99 per cent luck, and 1 per cent naked greed and opportunism.

The approved methods are as follows:

1) Getting in at the start of a £100 chain letter
2) Taking part in a Key Markets Scratch Away lottery
3) Winning a contract to supply fruit machines and video games to one of the oil states
4) Accidentally discovering that it is possible to make a commercially viable sausage out of reconstituted kangaroo meat and polystyrene ceiling tiles and proceeding to make a killing in the junk food business.

A Superwally, then, is a Wally who has struck it rich. But curiously, although all Wallies dream of one day breaking into the Superwally bracket, life as a Superwally is no bed of roses. On the contrary, it's extremely hard work – as you may begin to understand if for a moment you put yourself in the shoes of that get-rich-quick sausage king ...

Naturally your first step on acquiring your new-found wealth is to sell everything you own and move to a sprawling hacienda near Basingstoke complete with heliport and swimming pool especially built to your own design in the shape of a sausage. And that's when the trouble starts. Immediately news breaks that you've hit the big time, you find yourself being sponged upon by relatives, ripped off by supposed well-wishers and secretly resented by all and sundry. Your nearest neighbours in the mock-Tudor stud farm half a mile away make a point of not inviting you to their drinks parties. You're shunned at the tennis club. Worst of all, your family life beings to suffer. The wife moans and groans constantly about all the extra housework she's expected to do in your spanking new residence. You try and placate her by employing a team of Filipino servants to help out around the home, but it doesn't do any good; all she does now is complain they're nicking the silver – which indeed they are. Your kids too hate you for uprooting them from their old school and packing them off to a private establishment half a mile down a winding gravel drive somewhere in Ascot where they're forced to rub shoulders with a toffee-nosed collection of Jeremies, Jameses, and sons of High Commissioners and African potentates.

And as for *your* social life, on the rare occasions when you do get a chance to chew the fat with your old Wally pals, they seem less interested in talking over old times than in breaking bits off your furniture and removing your personal effects to take back and raffle in the pub.

Under the mounting pressure, you begin to hit the bottle in a big way. The wife, worried by your drinking and worn to a frazzle by more angry scenes with the Filipinos, votes with her feet and goes to stay with her mother in her mobile home in Worthing, leaving you to soldier on as best you can without her.

Plagued by visits from the Inland Revenue and by lurking

suspicions that your accountant is robbing you blind, your thoughts turn nostalgically to days gone by – days when you could spend a carefree evening chucking beer over the lads back at the Moon and Parrot and not have to stand drinks all round the moment you set foot inside the door. Haunted by bittersweet memories, you make a sentimental journey back to the pub you once knew and loved. But more disappointments are in store for you. The Moon and Parrot has vanished, its place taken by a giant hypermarket selling, amongst other things, the vile kangaroo and polystyrene sausages which you now curse yourself for ever having foisted on a gullible world. Sick at heart you return home to Southfork II and in a blind fury of wanton destruction tear the antique brass ornamental telephone out of its socket and put the boot into the wife's collection of Barry Manilow cassettes.

And now, on top of all the domestic grief and the boozing, financial problems begin to loom. On the advice of one of your Superwally friends you invest unwisely and lose your shirt on an abortive scheme for a night-club, casino and time-share apartment complex on a site adjoining the government weapons research establishment on Foulness. The debts begin to pile up. The months of high living – the lavish parties, the wrecked hotel rooms, the pranged limos and Aston Martins, the costly attempts to buy your eldest daughter a starring role in the latest Tim Rice-Andrew Lloyd Webber musical – all take their toll. And bit by bit the fairy tale fortune you amassed by a mixture of luck and sharp dealing in the sausage trade gets whittled away, until all you have left is a private hoard of Krugerrands which you're desperately trying to hide from the taxman.

Finally disaster strikes. Staggering down to breakfast in your towelling robe having demolished an entire bottle of banana liqueur with your early morning cup of tea, you find that a letter has been placed discreetly beside your usual pick-me-up of beaten egg, wheatgerm, brandy and Worcester Sauce by Bruno, your faithful eight-foot-tall deaf-mute manservant and minder.

With trembling fingers you tear open the envelope – but you already know in your heart that it contains dire news.

Sure enough. It's from your accountant, gloatingly informing you that he has absconded to Marbella taking with him not only the ravishing personal assistant and masseuse who was your only comfort over the last harrowing few months, but the entire contents of your wall safe.

Your life is in ruins. Or rather, it *would* be, were it not for one mysterious aspect of the Superwally phenomenon, namely that simply by being a Superwally you are an object of endless fascination to countless thousands of ordinary run-of-the-mill Wallies up and down the country.

Which explains why, just as you are taking a fond leave of Bruno and the Dobermans and preparing to take a farewell dip in your sausage-shaped swimming pool, one of the tabloids phones up out of the blue, offering half a million for the exclusive inside story of your marriage break-up, your heroic battle with the booze and your disastrous business ventures – and the whole grisly circus starts all over again ...

Moral: it may be tough where *you* are, down in the foothills of Wallydom, but it's even tougher for the Superwallies at the top.

WALLY REFERENCE

Important Dates in the Wally Year

1st January First hangover of the year

5th January 300 shopping days to Christmas

1st March Last chance to consume pre-Christmas Lyons Apple and Blackcurrant Sundaes

27th March Forget to put clocks forward

1st April Out with the laxative tea bags, Whoopee cushions, onion chewing gum and strap-on rubber boobs

8th April Buy new shirt in Spring Sale at C & A

9th April Lose it on Grand National

2nd May 200 shopping days to Christmas

27th August Bank Holiday. Load up motor with ghetto blaster, metal detector, roadside picnic kit and surfboard and head off to South Coast for the day …

28th August … forgetting that thousands of other Wallies have had exactly the same idea

30th August 100 Shopping days to Christmas

23rd October Forget to put clocks back

1st November Put up Christmas decorations

14th December Official start of Random Breath Test season

24th December Christmas Eve. Tear round shops in blind panic trying to buy all presents and provisions in last two hours of trading

25th December Break ice on Serpentine

26th December Pitch tent outside Selfridges

31st December Plunge into Trafalgar Square fountains wearing plastic motorway cone on your head

1. *Grandad* Clive Dunn
2. *There's No One Quite Like Grandma* St Winifred's School Choir
3. *Wombling Free* The Wombles
4. *Captain Beaky and his Band* Keith Michell
5. *Do you Think I'm Sexy* Rod Stewart
6. *Happiness* Ken Dodd
7. *The Deck of Cards* Max Bygraves
8. *Two Little Boys* Rolf Harris
9. *Making Your Mind Up* Bucks Fizz
10. *Perhaps Love* John Denver and Placido Domingo
11. *Save Your Love* Renee and Renato
12. *I Write the Songs that Make the Young Girls Cry* Barry Manilow
13. *Island in the Sun* Demis Roussos
14. *Viva Espana* Sylvia
15. *Superstar* Karen Carpenter
16. *Puppy Love* Donny Osmond
17. *Tie a Yellow Ribbon Round The Old Oak Tree* Dawn
18. *Hooked on Classics* The London Symphony Orchestra
19. *Fly The Flag* The 1982 England World Cup Squad
20. *The Birdy Song* The Tweets

Not all great smells come out of green plastic bottles in your bathroom cupboard. Don't miss the great smell of …

The changing rooms of the Tottenham Court Road Y.M.C.A.
A hot day in Dolcis
A warm summer's evening on the Kingston By-Pass
Burning clutch fluid
A long-distance lorry driver's sleeping bag
A roadie's singlet
A docker's armpit
Gillette Foamy Lemon and Lime Shaving Cream
A bouncer's shirtfront
Listerine Antiseptic Mouthwash
Scampi in the basket
Radian Warm-Up Sports Rub
Lavender air freshener and fried onions
Boiled fish and cabbage water
Low tide in the Bristol Channel
Midnight in Grimsby
The rear seats of the overnight coach to Glasgow
Tightly packed headbangers at a Status Quo gig

Wally Worldbeaters

A selection from The Wally Book of Records

The supermarket trolley found furthest from its supermarket of origin. Easily the world's most adventurous and well-travelled supermarket trolley is one originally belonging to the Dagenham Finefare fleet. It was hi-jacked by Wallies and later dumped among a container-load of washing-machine spare parts bound for Bahrain.

The longest Conga ever formed by Wallies at an office party. This record is at present held by the Staff Association of the National Westminster Bank who at their annual Xmas knees-up in 1982 managed to form a jubilant singing and dancing human chain consisting of over 3,000 staff members and occupying several floors of the Nat West building in London's Barbican. Eventually the Conga had to be broken up by police using riot shields, batons and water cannon.

The most outstanding contribution by a Wally to safe rail travel. This honour belongs to the unknown Wally in the British Rail design department responsible for devising the famous Inter-City hammer. This object, which has baffled thousands of commuters, can be found beside the window in every Inter-City rail-car and is clearly intended to be used by passengers in the event of a derailment to smash the windows and crawl out to safety. By a stroke of genius, the designer failed to provide any means of removing it from its glass case.

The least famous or noteworthy Wally ever to fit smoked glass windows on his Mini Clubman. Unfortunately the present record-holder is so obscure and ordinary that his name and career details aren't known.

KEEP BRITAIN WALLY

Members of The International Order of The Sick Parrot

Pam Ayres
Sue Barker
Tony Blackburn
Lionel Blair
Katie Boyle
Rhodes Boyson
James Burke
Billy Carter
Barbara Cartland
Richard Clayderman
Brian Clough
David Coleman
Perry Como
Robin Cousins
Paul Daniels
Val Doonican
Cyril Fletcher
Bruce Forsyth
Gary Glitter
Larry Grayson
Benny Hill
Fred Housego
Englebert Humperdinck
Instant Sunshine
David Jacobs
Tom Jones
Kevin Keegan
Eddie Kidd
Evil Knievel
Jonathan King
The Kings Singers
Bonnie Langford
Dave Lee Travis
Liberace
Little and Large
Barry Manilow
John McEnroe
Bob Monkhouse
Olivia Newton John
Des O'Connor
The Osmonds
Nicholas Parsons
Peter Powell
Victoria Principal
Esther Rantzen
Robin Ray
Ronald and Nancy Reagan
Kenneth Robinson
Erica Roe
Demis Roussos
Telly Savalas
Barry Sheene
David Soul
Arianna Stassinopoulos
Rod Stewart
Janet Street Porter
Denis Thatcher
John Travolta
Sir Hugh Trevor Roper
David Vine
Eddie Waring
Barbara Woodhouse
Jimmy Young
Lena Zavaroni

1 You will need:-
Bird's
Dream
Topping
1 packet Dream Topping
A large plastic bowl
Milk
2 Mix Dream Topping to 'sloppy' consistency
3 Bend over bowl, placing hands beneath it, so:-
4 Attempt to spin bowl through 360°....
5 .....Without sloshing it all down your front.

Party Pranks continued

The All England Wally Club

So you think you've got what it takes to be a Wally? Then why not join the All England Wally Club and take part in some of the exciting activities the Club has lined up for the coming year? A mass 'brew-up' outside the Department of the Environment as part of the Club's ongoing campaign for the legalisation of motorway picnicking. A coach excursion, available at specially reduced rates to Club members, to see the spectacular 'Son et Lumière Milton Keynes'. And not forgetting the Annual All England Wally Club Dinner in the car park of the National Exhibition Centre, Birmingham!

To apply for membership, simply study the form below then scribble *ET Phone Home* all over it and deface it exactly as you would a poster on the underground or any piece of time-wasting official-looking bumph.

I hereby declare that having taken on board all the advice contained in this lifesaver of a book I am now a fully fledged Wally. I agree to abide by the rules of the club although I understand that so far the committee have been too busy decorating the Club Headquarters with notices saying 'You don't have to be mad to work here but it helps' actually to get it together to write any. I enclose a cheque for £499.99, which I hope will cover everything.

The All England Wally Club Annual Dinner

I have a pretty good idea what's going to be on the menu of this year's dinner and I have decided:

- ☐ I'll risk it
- ☐ I'd rather be Hemeling
- ☐ I'd be better off at a Berni

Name ....

Address ....

SUPER WALLY!

INTRODUCTION

Wallies – they're all around us. From the Watford Gap Service Area, where they've taken the tops off the litterbins, put them on their heads and are now running around the car park pretending to be Daleks, to the Palace of Westminster, where they're busily trying to reduce the entire country to a state of complete Wallydom as quickly and expensively as possible – everywhere you look, the cult of the Wally has the nation in its grip.

Hardly surprising, then, that the question is being asked more and more frequently: what is a *Super*wally, and how do I become one?

The plain answer is that if learning how to be a Wally requires hours, days, weeks and even months of practice, then becoming a Superwally can take a lifetime – and even then, many still fail to make the grade.

Princess Anne, for example, seemed set fair to become one of the great Superwallettes of recent times – constantly swearing at journalists, pouting sulkily at photographers, falling off her horse at equestrian events ... But then, just as she seemed in line for a permanent place in the Superwally Hall of Fame, off she went, travelling round the Third World on behalf of the Save The Children Fund and making rather gamey jokes about lorry-drivers on the Australian Parkinson Show – hardly the behaviour of a potential Superwallette.

On the other hand, Mark Phillips has the distinct look of a major Superwally of the future. Not only does he make a habit of plunging head first into the waterjump at Badminton every year, but on those rare occasions when he actually manages to string a few words together, he invariably says the wrong thing – and with an effortless brilliance that immediately puts him yards ahead of the nearest competition.

But the dividing-line between success and failure in the Superwally stakes is perilously thin. To illustrate *how* thin, one need only point to the case of Tony Blackburn. Last year, he was looking like the ultimate Superwally DJ: Superwally jokes, Superwally false laugh, a regular Superwally show on Superwally Radio London. But then, one grim night in Kensington, he blew it all by responding with quiet and completely uncharacteristic dignity when a group of Ra-Ra Wallies led by Princess Di's Superwally brother tried to take his trousers down in a restaurant. Tony came up against bigger Superwallies than himself and found himself in what David Coleman would describe as All Sorts of Trouble. Result? Years of painstaking effort down the drain.

Then there was Neil Kinnock, who seemed a cert for Superwallydom when he fell flat on his back in the sea while posing for the cameras on his day of triumph in the Labour leadership contest. He was shaping up nicely – until he did something that no serious contender for Superwallydom would ever do: he tried to laugh it off and make a *joke* of it all.

So what does it take to become a Superwally?

Easy to sum up, but horribly difficult to achieve.

Superwallydom means being a Wally, and then some. It means, for example, staying up until three in the morning and phoning up K-tel simply to see if they really *do* operate a 24-hour ordering service. Or moving lock, stock and barrel to Crystal Palace in the hope of getting a better picture on your telly. It means queuing for days and then getting trampled underfoot in the stampede for Cabbage Patch Dolls in the January sales. Or wearing a hunting-knife strapped to your calf and genuine ex-Vietnam

GI combat jacket plastered with skull and crossbones and SAS insignia, then fainting at the sight of blood.

In other words, it means doing all the things a Wally would do, but then, just when everyone thinks you couldn't be more of a Wally if you tried, crowning it all by doing something so crass, so breathtakingly stupid it leaves your audience gasping with admiration.

For example, we all knew that Mark Thatcher was a Wally. But it wasn't until he got lost in the Sahara and brought half the Moroccan air force out looking for him that we realized he was a Superwally too.

We had all heard that President Chernenko was a bit of an old Wally, but it was only when he paused in the middle of his five-hour inaugural address as Soviet leader to allow the batteries in his pacemaker to recharge that we knew that he, like his opposite number in the White House, was a Superwally too.

Or take Hughie Green – obviously a Wally. But when he tried to film *Opportunity Knocks* on board a nuclear submarine to show his support for the government's defence policy, got the sack, then went around bleating that the Governors of the BBC and IBA were all part of the same gang and that they phoned each other up to say, 'Screw Hughie Green,' he exceeded the expectations of even his stoutest fans.

Likewise Prince Andrew. We all had him down as a Wally long ago; but when he sprayed white paint all over the international Press corps, then pretended his finger had slipped, he proved beyond any doubt that even in the face of some stiff competition from the rest of the family, he was far and away the biggest royal Superwally of them all.

And of course, we all had our suspicions that John Selwyn Gummer was a Wally, but it wasn't until recently that we saw how seriously we'd underestimated his talents. For when he revealed that he has the words SEX SEX SEX and YES YES YES emblazoned on his pillows and followed that by insisting that the Press drop the 'Selwyn' from his name, everybody did just that – and he's been John 'Superwally' Gummer ever since.

Can anybody become a Superwally?

By now it should be clear that there are some people in this world who start off with a significant advantage in the Superwally stakes. If, for example, you fall into one of the following categories, you should stand a better than average chance of successfully Going For The Big One:

- A member of the cast of *Coronation Street*
- An ex-mistress of a recently deceased comedian
- A football manager whose only scores are with other people's wives
- A brother or near-relation of Princess Di
- A team member on *A Question of Sport* (especially if you wear a diamond-patterned cardigan and engage in sickening banter with David Coleman)
- A sex-symbol from *Dallas* or *Dynasty*
- A guest on *The Price Is Right*
- An expatriate small-time villain living with a tubby peroxide blonde in Marbella
- One of the Nolan Sisters

INTRODUCING THE WALLETTE

There was a time, not so long ago, when any argument about equality between the sexes came down to the same old question: 'All right, then, if women are equal to men, how come there's not been one major female Wally in the whole of history?'

No one has ever been able to come up with a satisfactory answer. Some have put it down to lack of opportunity, others to a conspiracy on the part of male Wallies down the ages. Then again there were those who said that if Sir Arthur Bryant had been born female, our island story would have been given an entirely different slant.

But whatever the excuses, the fact remains: the way of the Wally has always been as truly masculine as the Great Smell of Brut.

Yet now, thanks to huge advances in social awareness, the daily efforts of countless Starbirds and Sun Page Three girls and, above all, the untiring leadership of such national figures as Pamela Stephenson, Erika Roe and Joan Collins, the serious business of being a complete and utter Wally is no longer exclusively a male preserve.

This is the age of the Wallette.

A Superwally should be able to spot the average Wallette immediately as she totters over the horizon on her platform heels, clutching her Snoopy bag and wearing her Duran Duran tee-shirt, but for mere Wallies who have not reached that level, here are her vital statistics:

Language

The Wallette's favourite words and phrases are 'out of order', 'winkle', 'the fellers', and 'You gotta laugh, eh?'

If you're not included in the above list, don't give up. By carefully studying this book you will gain comfort, inspiration and encouragement as you tread the long, lonely road ahead. But do bear in mind that Superwallydom can't be achieved overnight. Whether you choose to Go For The Big One by crossing the Atlantic in a bathtub, or pushing a supermarket trolley up Ben Nevis, remember: you *won't* be a Superwally if you succeed on the first attempt.

The Superwally Promise

Superwally! is a fully comprehensive guide which covers every aspect of the subject, from 'Little Wally's First Words' to 'The Art of Wally Seduction', on past 'Occupational Therapy for the Elderly Wally' to 'What to do with a Dead Wally's Ashes'.

And to show that the author and publishers of this book have complete confidence in its effectiveness in every case, we are prepared to offer a unique and unprecedented guarantee.

If any Wally, having bought a copy of *Superwally!* and read it thoroughly from beginning to end, genuinely believes that he has not become a Superwally as a result, then he has the right to return to the shop where he bought it and say, 'I have bought this copy of *Superwally!* and I can honestly say I'm as sick as a parrot, because frankly it just hasn't worked for me.'

The bookseller will then fall about laughing, and when he recovers, grasp him by the hand and say:

'Congratulations, son – you've made it at last!'

- Sitting around with other Wallettes in playgrounds, chewing bubblegum with her mouth open, talking about boys and swearing at children who ask her if please can she get off the swings now so they can have a go.
- Hanging around day after day outside the Radio One office in the vain hope of catching a glimpse of Peter Powell.
- Going to the disco and swaying around on the dance floor with another Wallette, staring into space, wishing a feller would come along and telling him to bog off when he does.
- Failing her driving test three times on the trot, even though she was showing most of her thighs the last time.
- Crying over a Mills and Boon romance at the launderette.
- Always carrying a toothbrush and a spare pair of knickers in her handbag just in case.
- Getting tiddly on port and lemon and then going on to a club to watch a male stripper, hooting with laughter and screaming, 'What d'you call that?' at the climax of his act.
- Going to Ann Summers coffee mornings and buying crotchless panties that she'll never dare wear.

Professions

Favoured Wallette professions include receptionist, barmaid, secretary, stripogram artiste, holiday tour guide topless waitress and prime minister. But without doubt the most popular career is that of Office Wallette.

The Office Wallette is usually from a temp agency, and has photographs of Lewis Collins, Nick Heyward and Prince William stuck over her desk beside a sign that says DON'T BLAME ME – I ONLY WORK HERE! Next to the typewriter lie:

1) A copy of *Honey* opened at the astrology page
2) An ashtray with a half-smoked, lipstick-stained Players No. 6 in it
3) A year's supply of nail varnish and false eyelashes
4) An *Over 21* address book filled with the phone numbers of endless other Wallettes

The Wallette will spend most of the day making phone calls to her Wallette friends, saying things like 'Then *he* said –' or 'I thought, cheeky sod, I thought –' or 'No, I couldn't, not just like that, not there, could I, no, well anyway I did –' or 'I could have *died*, honest, I've seen bigger matchsticks, I just didn't know where to look.'

Occasionally a Wally in the office makes the mistake of asking the Office Wallette out for a date. The next morning, she comes into the office smirking gruesomely at the other girls and crooking her little finger significantly.

Every year at the office party, the Office Wallette gets drunk and insults the managing director. A bit later she traps him in the car park and apologizes to him in floods of tears. As he backs away, seeking the safety of his Ford Granada, she launches herself at him with a French kiss, fails to make contact and hits the deck heavily as he speeds away. Later she invites the office junior to take her home and he's too frightened to say no. But once they get home, she passes out before anything can happen. The next morning her mind's a complete blank and she can't remember a thing about the previous evening.

Private Life

Just as the Wally spends most of his time Getting One Down, saving up for some Go-Faster stripes for his Escort and watching the wrestling on Saturday afternoon with the curtains drawn, surrounded by empty cans of Black Label and half-eaten packets of Monster Munch, the Wallette spends most of her time either thinking about, preparing for, or recovering from a night with 'the fellers'.

Although she is extremely active in this area, none of her relationships seem to last very long. This is because:

1) She is a Wallette
2) She goes out with Wallies
3) A change is as good as a rest, innit?

What sustains the Wallette through the hurly-burly of her less than satisfactory love-life is the fantasy that one night she'll be down at the Moon and Parrot with the girls after work, when she spots, sitting by himself in the corner, a face that seems strangely familiar to her. At that moment he glances up at her, almost shyly – and her heart misses a beat. Now she knows who he is. Those flashing green eyes. Those chiselled features. Those dark, flowing locks. It's what's-his-name from the smash ITV series for all the family *Robin of Sherwood.* He seems anxious to get away from the Moon and Parrot – after all, at any moment he could be recognized by one of his millions of fans. Muttering that she has to go and powder her nose she walks towards the door marked 'Hens'. As she does so, their eyes meet, as if to acknowledge the fierce, almost animal attraction for one another that they are both already feeling. Without a word he stands up. They walk out of the pub together. For a moment his hand softly touches her forearm as he opens the door of his gleaming white Lamborghini. She steps inside, settling back into the deep bucket seats, which smell intoxicatingly of real, expensive leather. There's the hint of a mischievous twinkle in Robin's green eyes as he smoothly eases the low-slung sports car into gear. 'Shall we

… go?' he whispers. And with a surge of power, pressing her deeper into her seat, Robin is soon whisking her away to his luxurious £150,000 Surrey mansion, where she will no longer just be a Wallette, but the mystery blonde who, my spies tell me, is now the live-in girlfriend and constant companion of TV's newest superstar …

In fact, the Wallette is not over-fussy about who finally rescues her from the leering Wallies at the Moon and Parrot, so long as he's famous and sexy. But she'd prefer it if he was one of the following:

1) Robin of Sherwood
2) Lewis Collins
3) Prince Andrew
4) Indiana Jones
5) The blond Wally in Wham
6) Jeremy Irons
7) Sting
8) Boy George
9) Peter Powell
10) Simon Le Bon

Superwallettes

The sad fact is that, unlike Wallies, Wallettes rarely have the staying power, the sheer dogged determination that it takes to Go For The Big One. Most reach a certain stage in their life when the fight goes out of them, they stop giggling and talking about winkles and become relatively normal.

On the other hand, there are a few Wallettes who are shining exceptions to the rule: Wallettes who have not only gone on to become Superwallettes, but who have actually built a career on their superb qualities in this area. Contrary to what many people think, this is not merely a question of appearing in front of the cameras as often as possible. Anna Ford clearly thought that was the case, but somehow has always failed to be a convincing Superwallette. Her Majesty the Queen, in spite of temptations that most of us would be unable to resist, has failed dismally in this regard. *We are not a Wallette ...*

Sarah Kennedy, too, was In All Sorts of Trouble when she moved from the Superwally show *Game For a Laugh* to *Sixty Minutes*, which was merely boring. In fact, it was beginning to look as if Sarah would never make the grade. But then she Went For The Big One, first by revealing that she was looking for someone to father a little Kennedy baby and then publicly changing her mind about the whole thing on television the following night – a sequence of events which won her the Order of the Sick Parrot in perpetuity.

Barbara Cartland and Barbara Woodhouse are natural Wallettes.* Joan Collins was almost certainly born a Wallette and finds it all as easy and natural as stripping off for *Playboy* at the age of fifty.

Then there's Pamela Stephenson, who should one day write a book about her heroic attempts to achieve Superwallettehood. At first, she appeared to have no chance when starring in *Not The Nine O'Clock News.* Then she started taking her top off in fashionable London restaurants and hiding under the table – classic Wallette behaviour. Unfortunately she suffered a major setback when she had a baby by Billy Connolly, who's nothing like a Wally. But now that she's once again appearing on the front of the *Daily Star* in a see-through blouse and silly dark glasses, it's beginning to look as if she's made it at last.

* Being called Barbara is undoubtedly an advantage if you want to be a Superwallette, as Barbaras Cartland, Woodhouse, Windsor, Bach (Ringo's Wallette) and Edwards prove. Interestingly, the name Ken, Kenny or Kenneth (as in Barlow, Everett, Lynch, Dalgliesh, Newman of the Yard and Robinson) confers a similar advantage on Wallies.

THE WALLY SUTRA

Throughout his life, every Wally finds himself a prey to all sorts of odd urges and strange, irresistible compulsions. The urge, for instance to press the little WAIT button on Pelican crossings, even when he hasn't the slightest intention of crossing the road; or to summon lifts in office blocks or department stores just for the hell of it; or, when at the cinema, to stand up just beneath the projectionist's box and entertain the rest of the audience by casting silhouettes of swans, ducks, flapping eagles or perhaps just his own thick head on the screen below. Nobody knows why he does these things – least of all him.

But without doubt the strangest and most baffling of all his compulsions is the mysterious desire that overcomes him once in a while to try and get off with a member of the opposite sex – even when bitter experience has taught him that this is the quickest known route to a slap in the face or a knee in the goolies, and that any successful docking-manoeuvre with a Wallette can be relied on to introduce all manner of hideous and unwanted complications into his life.

Since he's aware of the appalling pitfalls involved, the more circumspect Wally therefore does his best to ignore his troublesome sexual urges for as long as possible, and instead limits himself to the following tried and tested Wally sex substitutes:

1) He sidles up behind a likely-looking Wallette as she pores over a copy of *Oh Boy!* at the local John Menzies, pinches her bum, then either runs like hell or retires nimbly to a safe distance and pretends to be engrossed in the latest issue of *The Railway Modeller*.

2) He whistles at girls from the driving seat of his Capri, so that at the first sign of danger he can pull out from the

kerb and hare off down the road with a merry laugh and a squeal of tyres.

3) He leers down the barmaid's cleavage as she pulls him a pint, then goes 'GOORRRRR' with appropriate Wally body language while she rolls her eyes heavenwards and slouches off to serve another customer.

4) He plasters his motor with suggestive window stickers, e.g.:

- IF YOU FEEL SEXY, SMILE
- MAKE LOVE NOT WAR – SEE DRIVER FOR DETAILS
- FLASH YOUR LIGHTS IF YOU HAD IT LAST NIGHT
- SEX INSTRUCTOR – FIRST LESSON FREE

5) He moons out of coach windows at passing cars.

But eventually, of course, valuable as they are, these various forms of Wally para-sexual activity are no longer enough for him. The sinister stirrings from the region of his patterned nylon jockey briefs can no longer be denied. No matter how he fights it, sooner or later every Wally feels a need for the Real Thing.

In other words, he needs to Get A Bit.

Getting a Bit

If you've ever listened to a group of Wallies bragging about their sexual exploits as they hammer the Space Invader machine at the Moon and Parrot or dust themselves with great billowing clouds of Brut talcum powder in the locker room at the local sports centre, you might be forgiven for thinking that, as a would-be Wally Superstud, you're going to have to spend twenty-four hours of every day on the job. Nothing could be further from the truth. A quick fumble on the back seat of the motor every now and then is ample for most purposes – and, suitably embellished, it'll furnish you with raw material for quite enough outstanding tales of your superhuman sexual prowess to keep you going for at least three months, which, incidentally, is roughly how long it'll be before you start feeling your oats again.

Of course, that makes the whole business of Getting A Bit sound ridiculously simple – and it isn't. In fact, as any experienced Wally will know, it's considerably more complicated than it first appears – particularly in the uncut version of *Do You Come Here Often?*

So here to help you through those tricky early stages is a step-by-step guide to the art of Wally seduction, with real-life examples of the kind of problems you may encounter at each stage.

Step 1 What to wear when you're on the pull

First of all, when you're out combing the pubs and discos for the Wallette of your dreams, it pays to be correctly dressed. There's no accounting for taste, especially among Wallettes, and for some reason, the combination of a sweat-stained 'I'm With Stupid' T-shirt and a pair of sagging Levis that expose a half-moon of pink, spotty buttock every time you squat down to retrieve a dropped No. 6 coupon just isn't generally regarded as much of a turn-on.

No. You need Wally dress sense.

There are certain accoutrements that will mark you out immediately as a Wally of distinction. A St Christopher medallion is essential, obviously; so is a tight-fitting tailored shirt undone to the naval. And when it comes to the hardware, a good general rule is to load your fingers and wrists with as many chains, identity bracelets, Korean-made signet rings and Des O'Connor-style personalized diamanté cuff-links as you can manage without having to walk around with a permanent stoop – unless of course you're a happily married Wally looking for A Bit On The Side, in which case it's wise to leave the identity bracelet at home.

So you're now in full Wally combat gear, and you're hot to trot. A splash of the Great Smell of Brut behind each ear and half a pint down the jockey briefs for good measure and you're ready to go. But first, let's deal with a couple of common grooming problems.

STUD

'My problem is, I'm one very hairy guy – I mean, REALLY hairy! Last time I took a girl on a date, she accidentally brushed against me with a lighted cigarette and the whole of my chest went up in flames. I'm very worried about it as the lads at work all call me Godzilla and I'm afraid it could affect my chances with the girls.'

'Ape Man' of *Balham*

The rest of us should be that lucky. If there's one thing that's guaranteed to bring the Wallettes flocking, it's the sight of a broad, manly torso crowned with a luxuriant crop of bushy chest hair. Take no notice of your mates, they're just jealous – but maybe next time keep a pocket fire extinguisher handy for emergencies.

'I daren't go out on the pull because of this giant spot on my chin. I've tried everything but it just won't go away. Is there anything I can do? It's really making my life a misery.'

'Pimple' of *Enfield*

Short of having it surgically removed or burnt off with a blowtorch, the answer is No. But don't stay home moping about it – get out and find a Wallette with the same problem. That way you can spend hours discussing all the lotions, potions and patent remedies you've tried and you'll establish a valuable common bond for when the time comes to get down to cases.

Step 2 Finding a Wallette and making your move

Finding the kind of spot where Wallettes hang out isn't hard: every town has its cattle-market tucked away somewhere. It's getting a Wallette on her own that's the problem. Wherever you go, whether it's down at the pub or on the floor of the disco, you'll find that for some reason every available-looking female has a girlfriend in tow who looks at best like a member of the Russian Olympic weight-lifting squad and at worst like an extra from a Fellini movie – and sometimes the two of them are so inseparable you begin to wonder if you're going to have to pour coconut oil all over them and prise them apart with a crowbar.

If the five most beautiful words in the English language are 'Buy one, get one free', the six most deadly have *got* to be 'Mind if my friend comes too?' So make sure you have a game-plan for precisely this situation: a range of stylish opening gambits designed to sweep the Wallette of your choice right off her feet and force her to ditch Number Two at the earliest opportunity. For example:

'Hey, where have you been all my life?'
'Hey, has anyone ever told you you look just like the dark one in Bananarama?'
'Hey hey hey, you're a big girl. Ever thought of doing a centrefold for my mates at *Penthouse*?'
'Pinch me – I think I'm dreaming!'

The rest is plain sailing – or it should be …

'I keep on seeing this amazing girl down at the local disco and I really fancy her something rotten. I'm sure I've seen her somewhere before: maybe in a magazine, or on TV – maybe even in a past life …?

'I long to pluck up courage to talk to her, but I can tell she's not like all the other girls and I'm afraid of making a fool of myself. What should I do?'

'Lovesick' of *Luton*

You should get one thing straight for a start: unless you're a top-class Superwally like Prince Andrew, Mark Thatcher or Oliver Reed, you're never going to Get A Bit with models, debs or TV personalities. If God had meant you to score with the Anna Fords and Selina Scotts of this world, he'd have given you a receding chin, a private income and a fleet of brand-new BMWs.

You're a Wally. Your only chance of success is with a Wallette. It's tough, but that's life.

> *'I've never had any problem chatting up the girls. My trouble is, whenever one of them reaches past me for her handbag or brushes against me on the floor I get so excited I have an accident in my Y-fronts. Is this what's known as premature ejaculation and if so, is there a cure?'*
>
> *'Hair-trigger'* of *Harlow*

Sadly, this is a common problem and there's not much you can do about it except to try and concentrate on something else until the danger's passed. Try thinking about something really boring to take your mind off it. The SDP's chances in the next election, the Public Sector Borrowing Requirement, Bobby Robson's use of the 4-2-4 formation in the Big One against Luxembourg, or, if all else fails, try remembering the name of your Euro-MP.

Step 3 The Crunch

Once you've managed to extricate your chosen Wallette from the melée of gyrating bodies and you've screamed a few endearments into her ear above the blare of the jukebox or PA, you're then faced with a tricky decision. Where's it to be? Round the back for a quick one, and face the usual 11.15 bottleneck? The back seat of the motor, and risk attracting the attention of other Wallies, who'll leer through the window, hammer on the roof and put you off your stoke by going 'Waauurrrr!' or yelling other forms of ribald encouragement from the pavement outside? Or back to your place, where you'll be expected to engage her in time-wasting conversation about star signs, the boss's BO, what Boy George said to Wogan on telly the other night, and apologise for the embarrassing beer and TV dinner stains on the sheets?

Let's assume it's the latter. And now comes the really difficult part: the actual act of Getting A Bit.

One of the major causes of sexual maladjustment among Wally couples these days is the assumption on the part of the Wally that every Wallette is up and ready and raring to go as quickly as he is. On the contrary: she needs a fair bit of coaxing, wheedling and general tuning up before she's in the mood.

So instead of launching yourself at her with a cry of GERONIMO-O-O-O!!! the moment you get inside the front door, show a bit of consideration: pause, count to ten, and ply her with a piece of traditional Wally foreplay, e.g.:

'Right – get 'em off then.'

Then switch off the lights, clamber on top of her and let Nature take its course.

> *'I thought my luck was in the other night when I saw this gorgeous bird winking at me from over the other side of the room at this party at my mate Wally's. But when I took her back to my place for a quick bonk, she got into a right state and started going on about how she was fed up with being treated as a sex object and how men were only interested in one thing and wouldn't it be nice if once in a while instead of trying to prove how bloody virile they were they'd just sit you down in the kitchen like any normal human being and have a cup of tea and a chat.*
>
> *'What I want to know is: Where did I go wrong?'*
>
> *'Puzzled'* of *Peasedown*

Human sexual relations are a complex thing, and in the course of that infinitely subtle, infinitely suggestive interplay that makes up the Wally mating ritual, it's all too easy to misread the signs – especially when you've staggered round every pub and disco in town in search of a bit of spare and you're so pissed you can hardly stand up. So, be warned; don't mistake a 'Hands off' for a 'Come hither'. It's very tempting to believe that the girl making eyes at you across the dance floor is panting for a night of steamy passion, when in fact all she's doing is trying to dislodge a piece of grit from her contact lens.

> *'When it comes to sex, I've always reckoned I was as broadminded as the next man, but the other night I don't mind telling you I got the shock of my life. I was just getting down to basics with this bit of fluff I'd picked up outside the chippie, when all of a sudden she stops and says, "Hang about. I know a different way. Why don't we try it with me on top." I showed her the door right sharpish, I can tell you! But then later I started wondering: I mean, it did sound a bit ... well, you know,* kinky *– but so what? Supposing she had a point there? Did I do the right thing?'*
>
> *'Strangeways'* of *Streatham*

The answer to this is that as every Wally knows, there's really only one Wally love position: it's called the One Over The Eight, and it involves the Wallette lying flat on her back with one eye on the clock in case she misses the last bus and the other on the letters page in *Honey*, while you're spreadeagled on top of her, desperately trying to husband your energies so that you don't pass out in a drunken stupor in mid-performance.

But on the other hand, if being a Wally stud means anything at all, it means notches on bedposts – and whether you choose to Get A Bit standing up, lying down or swinging from a chandelier, a score is still a score.

Step 4 The Follow-Through

It's commonly supposed by most newcomers to the art of Wally seduction that by this stage you're home and dry: that all that remains is to scrub the lipstick off your collar, take a quick shower followed by another thorough dousing with the Great Smell of Brut to disguise any lingering whiffs of Body Mist, 4711 or poncy Menthol cigarettes, then hurry back down to the pub or wherever to give the lads an in-depth blow-by-blow post-match commentary.

If only life were that simple. In fact, in nine cases out of ten what happens is that instead of basking in the afterglow, you now have to weather a storm of tears and recriminations as the Wallette launches into either:

> *'You won't tell my Dad will you promise you won't tell my Dad he'd bloody kill me if he found out'*
>
> or:
> *'Am I on the pill what do you mean am I on the pill that's bloody typical of a man that is of course I'm not on the pill what kind of a girl do you take me for'*
>
> or:
> *'You bloody men you're all the same you're only interested in one thing I suppose it's never occurred to you a girl has feeling* oh *no a quick leg-over that's all you're after and anything in a split-seam skirt and platform heels is fair game well I'll tell you something big boy we're not all brainless dollybirds you know we're not all like that fat tart Lesley* oh *yes I saw you giving her the eye so don't you come the little innocent with me we're not all silly bits of fluff you can pick up and chuck away when the fancy takes you and there is such a thing as respect you know course I don't suppose you'd know the meaning of the word and you needn't think just because a girl lets you touch her up in the carpark it means she wants to leap into oi I'm talking to you and you can put away that dirty mag too if you don't mind you know something your type really make me want to throw up you and your tight trousers and your mirror shades and your hullo darlings and your gold bloody chains and your Ford bloody Cortinas you really fancy yourself don't you you really reckon you're a stud well let me tell you something I've had more fun staring at a crack in the wall you're all bloody mouth that's your trouble course I blame myself I mean I should have*

known I don't know why I bloody fall for it it's the same every time I must need my bloody head examined ...'

It all underlines the central timeless paradox at the heart of the Wally mating game, namely that only a complete and utter Wally would ever attempt to Get A Bit with a Wallette. On the other hand, only a Wallette would let him.

You just can't win.

WALLY FAMILY LIFE

At a certain age – say in his mid-to-late twenties – the average Wally begins to feel that there's more to life than motors, Carling Black Label and *The Price is Right.* He wonders whether at his age he ought not to be looking for something more lasting, more meaningful and life-enhancing than simply pushing other Wallies around the shopping-precinct carpark in supermarket trollies every Saturday afternoon. He may even ask himself whether the time has come for him to think of someone other than himself, of his long-term future and prospects.

At this point, more often than not, he'll pull himself together, say 'On yer bike, my son – time to Get One Down you' and adjourn swiftly to the Moon and Parrot, where a bunch of other Wallies, who like as not have also just experienced the same painful microsecond of introspection and self-doubt, are already Going For It and are on their second pint. And usually that's the end of that.

But then sometimes, as he listens to Wally from down the road telling his one Little and Large joke for the third time that night, as he laughs dutifully and says, 'Like it, like it,' with all the other lads, he suffers another twinge of unease.

What could be wrong? The lads are there. They've all got enough down them now to have a rowdy game of darts and sing along with *Sailing* on the jukebox, leer at a few Wallettes, then go out to the car park and throw the litter bins about. So why this strange feeling that there should be more to life than this?

The answer is that being a complete and utter Wally all the time simply isn't enough for him any more. He secretly hankers after intimate evenings watching *Terry and June* on the Sonyvision, cuddled up in front of the safe and economical Living Flame natural gas fire. He dreams of building utility sheds in the back garden with shiny Black and Decker tools, now and then biting into a Mars Bar, while his own little Wallette watches him fondly from the kitchen window, where she's doing the washing up again. He pictures himself trudging up the garden path with a sunny smile and muddy boots and asking, 'What's for lunch, love?' while she shakes her head, ruefully eyeing the great clods of earth he's just brought into the house and says brightly, 'Birds Eye Cod Fillets, of course,' and he smiles again and starts tucking in while she contentedly mops up the muddy floor ...

In other words, he wants a home, a wife and, above all, the chance to make lots of Little Wallies.

And just to make sure there are no problems in the Little Wally department, the average Wally usually gets his Wallette in the club well before the topic of marriage is broached. This has the added advantage of making it look as if his rampant need to Get A Bit at all costs has caused him to be forced into marriage by family and other pressures. Because of course, no serious Wally should ever admit to his mates that he actually *wants* to settle down and raise a family.

Settling Down

Just because the Wally now has a better half, there's absolutely no reason why his basic lifestyle should change significantly in any way whatsoever. It's possible that for a few months he won't feel the need to go 'Gooorr!' whenever a Wallette walks by, but after a while, even this habit will return and life will go on much as before.

Until, that is, the arrival of Little Wally.

Bringing up Little Wally

Some people are born Wallies (one thinks immediately of Jeremy Beadle, Cyril Smith and Jonathan King), some achieve Wallydom (Torvill and Dean, John Selwyn Gummer), and some have Wallydom thrust upon them (anyone selected to represent Great Britain in the Eurovision Song Contest). But unless you're utterly convinced that you've produced a born Wally (and these are still relatively rare), then it's wise to give Little Wally every chance in life by bringing him up to be at least as big a Wally as you are, and if possible a bigger and better one too. Fail to make that effort and literally anything could happen: a scholarship to Oxford at the age of twelve, good works among the starving millions of the Third World, a brilliant career with the Royal Shakespeare Company, or worse.

Remember – you can't start too early.

The first months

In these early months, it's simply a matter of peering into his cot when you come back from the Moon and Parrot and making as many quintessentially Wally faces or noises as you can manage without giving yourself more of a headache than you have already. Child psychologists have confirmed that the sight of a huge, friendly face with unfocussed, bloodshot eyes and crisp crumbs around the mouth, and the familiar smell of Watney's Red Barrel as it wafts over the cot can have a formative influence on the very young.

But bear in mind that even Little Wally has a brain, however miniscule. So gradually move from making friendly Wally noises – 'Goooorrr!', 'We-haay!', 'Oroight?' and 'Whaaaat?' – to actual words and phrases. There can be no greater thrill in family life than hearing Little Wally mouth his first words. If you have been relating to him in the correct way, they should be one of the following:

'Like it'
'Magic'
'Nice One'
'Tasty, tasty'
'On yer bike'
'Come on you Spurs'
'Wallee' (pointing at you)
'Yer jooookin'

The early years

It is absolutely vital that Little Wally learns to express himself, develops his own character, discovers his own strengths and weaknesses, fights his own fights and becomes an individual Wally in his own right as early as possible. At the same time, it's also absolutely vital that he avoids doing any of this while you're trying to watch *Crossroads*, cracking open a few cans of lager with the lads while the wife's out shopping, having a meal or doing the pools.

So Little Wally will need a sense of discipline – some basic rules to live by:

1) Whenever he makes any kind of noise or tries to speak, say 'Shut up, you!' and ignore him. Many of the best brought up Little Wallies can reach the age of six or seven still believing that their name is Shutupyou.
2) When the lads come round for a drink, don't make him feel left out: give him a can of Black Label too. At first, he'll just mess around with the ring top – the tricks he learns now will serve him in good stead at the office party in a few years' time – but after a while he'll start imitating you: Getting One Down, smacking his lips noisily and lisping, 'It's what your right arm's for'.
3) Encourage him to make his presence felt at the local play group by knocking over other children's piles of

bricks, asking the Little Wallettes if he can see their bottoms, leaving a Farley's rusk soaked in milk on the play-leader's chair and nutting the other little Wallies for no particular reason. Once in a while you may find he's been nutted back by one of them, in which case you should pay a visit to the Daddy of the Little Wally responsible and threaten to push his teeth so far down his throat he'll have to stick a toothbrush up his bottom to clean them.

4) Always make him climb the highest slides in the playground. If he succeeds, it'll show he's got bottle – as important a quality for a little Wally as for a big one. If he doesn't and falls flat on his head from a great height, don't worry: it'll probably improve his chances of growing up to be a complete and utter Wally no end.

5) Never encourage him to mix with little girls who may already have discovered that one of their missions in life is to cramp the style of Wallies, be they little or big. On the other hand, if he insists on inviting some little Wallettes round for tea now and then, don't panic, but refer to his prowess down at the pub later, e.g.:

'Gor, you should see my Little Wally – he can't half pull the birds! Had three of them round at our place today. Going to be a right little tearaway, he is.'

'Chip off the old block, eh?'

'This is it.'

Some early signs of Wallydom in the young

Every Wally father remembers that proud moment when, through some particularly ignorant or moronic word or deed, his son proves that he's got what it takes to Go For The Big One. All your efforts were worthwhile: Little Wally's going to Get It Right.

There are endless tell-tale signs for the watchful parent. For example:

- He falls asleep face-down in a bowl of Milupa.
- He swallows his dummy.
- He treads on a Carling Black Label can and clunks up and down the street with it bent around his foot.
- He ties all the swings together in the playground so that it takes the park attendant half an hour to untangle them.
- He writes WALLY 4 TRACY on the bus shelter when he doesn't even know a Tracy.
- He goes round to other little Wallies' houses while their parents are away to watch the latest video nasties.
- He does wheelies on his BMX bike and falls flat on his back.
- He charges into a game of football being played by kids at least five years younger than him and scores ten goals, doing a John Motsom imitation at the top of his voice.
- He cuts out *Sun* Page Three girls and keeps them in his bottom drawer but doesn't really know why.
- He starts collecting highly toxic novelty rubbers in the shape of biscuits and liquorice allsorts and offering them round to all his friends.
- He wins £5 and a Reporter's Certificate by getting a letter published in the 'What's Your View?' column in the *Junior TV Times*. E.g.:

  'I used to enjoy Game For a Laugh *I thought it was brilliant, it was all comedy and fun, I wish it was back on telly. Matthew Kelly was great and so was Jeremy Beadle as well.* Fraggle Rock *is good too it is so enjoyable and interesting that even our dog Biff sits down and watches it. Everyone can fall in love with the cute little doozers except my dad of course he is usually asleep then.'*

  'Fragglefan' (10) Humberside.

DO NOT FEED
THE LIONS
P.B.
RELAX
STAR WARS

DO NOT EAT
THE WALLIES

Toys

The most important thing about Little Wally's toys is that you should be able to enjoy playing with them when he's at school or asleep. There's not much fun to be had from a Baby Bouncer or Postman Pat video, but you can get hours of enjoyment from riding around on a baby's first tricycle.

Other toys worth investing in are:

- A climbing frame which collapses under your weight
- A Steve Davis mini-snooker set
- An Eric Bristow Junior Dartboard
- A Colonel 'H' Action Man
- A BMX bike
- A large-scale Build-Your-Own Cruise Missile set, complete with transport vehicle.

Little Wallettes

There's no getting away from it: even in this day and age it's considerably more difficult to bring up real little Wallettes than real little Wallies. So, when the Wally father discovers that the tiny creature he's been dandling on his knee for the past two years is a girl, not a boy, he'll probably mutter something about it being a Bit of a Choker When All's Said And Done and take no further interest. Until, of course, she starts going out with a boyfriend, when he'll look up from the television and say something to the effect of: 'If that idle layabout gets you into trouble, you're out on your ear, girl – I kid you not.'

However, for the Wally who prefers to play a more active part in bringing up a right little Wallette, there are two basic rules to remember:

1) Get her a bra and makeup set as soon as she's out of nappies.
2) Put her down for an audition with *Minipops* before her fifth birthday.

WALLY'S BEST FRIEND

There's absolutely nothing wrong in wanting to keep a pet if you're a Wally. But remember – many an instant character appraisal has been formed on the basis of what pet you own, so Get It Right. No one will take you seriously as a Wally if, for example, you wander around a shopping precinct with a peregrine falcon on your shoulder and a couple of pedigree pointers trailing along behind you.

Choosing a pet that will enhance your status among other Wallies is a tricky business, but here are some basic guidelines:

Pets a Wally can be seen with
An Alsatian
A Doberman Pinscher
A greyhound or whippet
An English Mastiff
Any large, stupid-looking mongrel
A ferret
A parrot that says 'Nice one, Cyril'
A goldfish for Little Wally

Pets a Wally should never be seen with
A thoroughbred racehorse
A polo pony
A golden eagle
A golden retriever
Any kind of big cat
Any kind of domestic cat
A labrador
A rabbit
A gerbil

Some Wallies have made a bold bid for originality by keeping pairs of miniature poodles, naming them Dot and Carrie or Benson and Hedges, and dressing them up in neat little tartan coats for when the weather turns chilly. On the whole, though, it's advisable to play safe and go for a large, ugly, potentially dangerous brute that's guaranteed to put the fear of God into postmen and Old Age Pensioners and leave nice big turds in people's front gardens.

Naming your Wally Pet

This is relatively straightforward. All Wally pets should of course be male – in fact, they should as unmistakably and impressively male as possible – so the range of names you have to choose from is somewhat limited.

Avoid anything amusing, fancy or clever. Go for something with true Wally style, plus a hint of thoroughly masculine menace, e.g.:

Biff
Starsky
Clint
Gnasher
Rex
Tebbit
Gummer

Training your dog the Wally way

Don't bother about training the brute when he's inside the house, apart from administering the odd kick whenever he's in range and beating him soundly if he farts during mealtimes. And don't overfeed him either – that rangy, ribby look as he tugs ferociously on his choke-chain will earn you impressed looks from the other Wallies on your street. Training your dog the Wally way involves:

1) Brutalising and humiliating him by lengthy and pointless sessions in the park: you on one side, yelling

'*Stay, Biff!*' at the top of your voice; Biff rummaging around in a litter bin three hundred yards away, taking not a blind bit of notice.

2) Encouraging him to mate energetically with anything in sight – cushions, chair legs, lamp-posts, Jehovah's Witnesses, Avon ladies, etc.

3) Allowing him to let off steam by rushing up to small children, snarling and baring his teeth. As the child is led away in hysterics, laugh and tell the parent he's just being friendly.

4) Dressing him up in a bow tie and a paper hat, sitting him on a piano stool, filming his performance on video and sending it off to *That's Life*.

THE WALLY AND THE IVY

There can be few more magical moments in the Wally family calendar than the arrival at long last of the season of Black Carling, Good Beer and random Breath Tests: Yuletide.

Everything is prepared. The decorations have been up since the beginning of November. The little silver Christmas tree is laden with those candles, baubles and fairies that weren't smashed to pieces during last year's New Year's Eve party. There's a MERRY XMAS sign on the front door just under the plastic Santa which you bought from Woolworths four years ago and which now looks more like Frankenstein's monster. There's a keg of bitter in the corner and some sparkling wine in the fridge for the day itself. The wife's parents have settled into the usual pre-Christmas torpor and are already complaining about the way Little Wally exposes himself out of the front window to passers-by. The hangover from the office Christmas party is now little more than a distant buzzing in the ears and there have been no embarrassing phone calls, so presumably that little episode in which you gave the Wallette from accounts your number after checking out her bottom line down behind the photocopier must have been a figment of your imagination.

Mrs Wally is already a bit giggly because she's been Getting It Down Her in the kitchen with the cooking sherry, which was meant for the trifle. Little Wally is Over The Moon because he's sure he's going to get a BMX bike at last.

You're primed and ready for the perfect Wally Christmas.

CREME DE MENTHE
BRUT
TV TIMES
P.B.

Some really magic Christmas presents, together with the thoughts that count

From Mum to Dad:

A power tool kit. ('Hope he drills a hole through his bloody foot.')

From Dad to Mum:

A Marks and Spencers Summer Gift Voucher. ('I warned her I didn't have much time to buy presents, didn't I?')

From Dad to Little Wally:

A model Dinky Toy BMX bike. ('Didn't say how big it was going to be, did I?')

From Mum to Little Wally:

A Radio One 'Hullo Mate' badge. ('Thank you, Peter Powell.')

From all the Wallies to Granpa:

A Starbird Calendar. ('That should keep him happy, the randy old so-and-so.')

From all the Wallies to Granma:

Winifred Atwell's Christmas Party. ('Serves her right for giving it to *us* last year.')

From Granma and Granpa to Dad:

Six cans of alcohol-free lager. ('Not that he'll take the hint, the Wally.')

From Granma and Granpa to Mum:

A Baby's First Words Album. ('Well, it's not right Little Wally being all on his own like that.')

From Granma and Granpa to Little Wally:

A BMX bike. ('That'll show the poor little beggar what tight parents he's got.')

- Guess how far into *The Sound of Music* Granma will fall asleep and start snoring.
- Guess which is going to come first: 'The Hills are Alive With The Sound Of Music' or Granma waking up with a start when her false teeth fall out.
- Think up an original excuse for leaving the family and nipping down to the Moon and Parrot where all the other Wallies will be singing 'The Twelve Days of Christmas'.
- See how many items of furniture you can smash while trying out Little Wally's BMX in the sitting room.
- Try to find the duff bulb on the Christmas tree lights in under two hours.
- Guess what Mrs Wally got mixed up with the brandy that makes the Christmas pudding taste so odd.
- Guess who'll be the first to say *either* 'I remember when Christmas used to be a real family occasion' *or* 'It's not the same without Eric and Ernie' *or* 'Next year we're going to spend Christmas in a hotel in Margate and have done'.
- Guess when, and on whom, Little Wally will bring up the entire box of Milk Tray he's been scoffing on the quiet.

- 'I don't know why you lot don't go to church like we did when we were young – it *is* His bloody birthday today in case you hadn't noticed.'
- 'If certain members of this family who shall remain nameless had lifted a *finger* to help in the kitchen instead of sitting around getting drunk, you'd have *got* Christmas dinner before four o'clock.'
- 'It *is* a turkey – it just shrunk a bit in the oven.'
- 'No, that's just way out of order, Granpa. I do not invite you to spend Christmas in my home just to have you stinking the place out after the Christmas pudding.'
- 'We know you want to watch *Where Eagles Dare* but Mummy wants to watch *The Sound of Music* and Christmas is Mummy's day, isn't it?'
- 'I don't care if Daddy does want to watch *Where Eagles Dare* – he's done sod all to help today so you can all bog off down to the park for a couple of hours 'cos I'm watching bloody Julie Andrews so there.'
- 'I hate Christmas I hate Julie Andrews I hate turkey I hate you all and I'm going to smash you all with my BMX bike and then I'm going to smash my BMX bike too.'
- 'He's not a spoilt little brat and if you and Granma don't like it here you can bog off back to the home for all I care and don't bother to come back next Christmas, you geriatric old git.'
- 'Don't you abuse my father like that, you ignorant Wally, or I'll tell everyone about a certain call I had yesterday from a certain someone in Accounts who had a certain experience down behind the photo-copier at a certain office Christmas party, you randy old sod.'
- 'I still say there was no need to throw the remains of the turkey all over the carol singers.'

THE COMPUTER WALLY

Not even the most uninformed Wally can fail to have noticed that this country is currently in the grip of a major technological revolution. New industries are sprouting up, old ones are going to the wall. Everywhere you look, it's micro-this or micro-that. Even in the shops, the comforting jingle of the old-fashioned cash register is being replaced by the electronic chirrupings of the latest computerised check-out till. Like it or like it not, it looks as if the Mighty Micro is here to stay.

So it seems reasonable to pose the question: what impact is all this having on the Wally in the street?

Well, as far as the vast mass of ordinary run-of-the-mill Wallies are concerned, the answer is: depressingly little. Along with ninety per cent of the rest of the population, most Wallies are unashamed Luddites who only come into contact with the New Technology once a year when they spill half a gallon of Black Label over the firm's computer at the office party. And of course you only have to mention the words Silicon Chip for one of them to chime in with the obligatory joke about this Irish geezer who went into this shop and asked for one so they gave him one in a bag and he said hang about where's the salt and vinegar geddit ber-boom HURR-HURR-HURRR. It's a sad fact that probably the first time the computer boom impinged on the consciousness of the average Wally was when the manager at the local W.H. Smith's rearranged the magazine racks to make room for all those glossy computer journals – the result being that *Auto-Car, Bike, Men Only* and *New Directions* were banished to the top shelves and Joe Wally found himself having to stand on a step ladder to read them.

But among a small, perhaps more forward-looking section of the Wally population, things were rather different. Never slow to jump on a bandwagon, this advanced breed of Techno-Wallies soon realized that, properly used, the computer brought with it a golden opportunity to waste more time more pointlessly and cause bigger and better administrative cock-ups than at any previous point in human history. They perceived the simple truth: that just as every home, office or small business would one day have its own computer, so each home, office or small business would one day have its very own resident *Computer Wally*.

How to become a Computer Wally

Before the advent of the home computer, Computer Wallies were a rare and élite breed to be found only in the bosoms of large corporations and the accounts departments of the nationalized industries. And so, for many years, the incomparable thrill of accidentally wiping off the entire divisional sales figures for the past three years, playing frisbee with a collection of floppy discs, or adding a couple of extra noughts to an Old Age Pensioner's gas bill was only vouchsafed to a privileged few.

But thanks to the recent boom in small, inexpensive home computers and the fact that Dragons, Nords, Spectrums and the like are now falling off the backs of lorries up and down the country, Computer Wallydom has at last come within the reach of all – and at a cost roughly equivalent to no more than a few nights' serious drinking down at the Moon and Parrot.

Step 1 Buying your Home Computer

This is not nearly as difficult as it sounds – so chuck away all those computer mags and 'Which Computer' colour supplement pull-out guides for a start. Basically it all boils down to a question of *either*

a) Going for a dirt-cheap TI-99 and then finding there's no software to go with it. *Or*

b) Splashing out a whole week's beer money on one of the really pricey models and then finding that if there *is* any software to go with it, you can't afford it.

Step 2 Teething troubles

By the time you've installed your Wallytron 2000, spent hours trying to figure out how to program it, taken out your frustration on the wife, kids, Alsatian and anybody else within range, and finally given up on it and stormed off to the Moon and Parrot with a splitting headache, leaving the computer to the tender mercies of Little Wally (who, needless to say, mastered it weeks ago with effortless aplomb), you may well be tempted to ask yourself why you bothered to buy the bloody thing in the first place.

And you won't be the only one, either. Your mates will probably be asking you the same question. Don't be thrown by this: even the most accomplished Computer Wally occasionally comes in for a bit of good-natured ribbing from the lads. Simply silence them with one of the following carefully prepared and totally specious stock answers:

	Rough Translation
I mean, after all, basically it's the computer age, innit?	*Next door's got one.*
I mean, I didn't want Little Wally to miss out, did I?	*I thought it'd keep Little Wally off the streets.*
I mean, you've got to think of the kid's future, haven't you?	*Honest, I had to do something – it was that or Borstal.*
'Course, it's not a toy.	*'Course, to him it's just a toy.*
It's *educational.*	*I don't know why I bothered.*

He's learning these amazing things off it.

All the little bastard does all day is sit in front of it, crash-landing Jumbo Jets.

Taken to it, like a duck to water, he has.

I just can't get him off the bleeding thing.

He's even using one at school now.

It's the same at school.

That's what it's all about really – it's, like, training him to take his place in the society of the future.

It's a bloody waste of the taxpayers' money, if you ask me. At this rate the only qualification that kid's going to end up with is a CSE in bloody Space Invaders.

'Course, I'm getting to grips with it meself now.

'Course, I'd use it meself only I haven't got two brain cells to rub together.

It's ever so useful in the home.

You can do the Pools on it, you know.

And the beauty of it is, *all the family can get involved.*

Trouble is, what with Little Wally and his Jumbo Jets and Granpa hooked on VIOLENT UNIVERSE, I can't get a bloody look in.

See, it's user-friendly – even a child of four can work it.

Stone me, even the wife's had a go.

Step 3 Getting the Best out of your Wallytron 2000

Having overcome the early difficulties, every Computer Wally now experiences a momentary pang of guilt: here, sitting on his breakfast bar, is a highly sophisticated piece of electronic hardware – and so far he's failed to use it for anything more demanding or intellectually stimulating than the odd game of PSST!, Pac-Man or Asteroids. So after many, many painful hours dinning into his skull the rudiments of computer programming, he now finds he has to wrack his brain to think of some potentially more worthwhile use to which to put it.

Mercifully, this stage is short-lived, but to carry you over it, here are a few ideas:

- Logging the Alsatian's feeding times.
- Running a private computer-dating scheme.
- Providing up-to-the-minute details of the current state of your account with Take Six, Harry Fenton, MFI and Augustus Barnett.
- Plotting the wife's biorhythmic cycle.
- Calculating the mother-in-law's life expectancy.
- Attempting to access top-secret Ministry of Defence data-banks for details of the latest cruise missile deployments, then trying to flog the story to the *Guardian.*
- Keeping a computerized record of the previous season's racing results, so you can tell at the press of a button whether it's worth risking a fiver on Golden Boy at 15 to 1 in the 2.30 at Newmarket.

But of course, a computer is only as good as the information you feed into it. And after you've spent an entire evening tapping on to the computer a list of all the people you plan to send Christmas cards to, only to find that when you call up the results on the screen they're totally unintelligible because you were half pissed at the time and got all the addresses muddled up, you may well find that disenchantment begins to set in again. At which point it's high time to cut your losses and resign yourself to the fact that basically you're going to end up using your computer just the same way as every other Computer Wally from Land's End to John O'Groats. In other words, you're going to play games on it.

Step 4 A Brief Guide to some Wally Computer Games

Given the vast range of mind-bogglingly tedious Computer Games on the market, you should have no difficulty here. Simply select two or three of the more spectacularly Wally ones and you'll soon find yourself becoming so hooked on them that you're as dependent for survival on your hourly dose of JET SET WILLY as a junkie screaming for his fix.

In fact, it won't be long before all normal family life goes by the board, those carefree nights puking your guts up in the car park of the Moon and Parrot are nothing but a distant memory, and you're plugged into your Wallytron twenty-four hours a day, red-eyed and unshaven, zapping away like a Wally possessed, while the tempting plateful of turkey burgers and oven chips which the wife brought you three days ago before finally gathering up her belongings and decamping to her mother's, kids and all, lies mouldering disregarded at your elbow. There's no hope for you now. You're beyond all human recall. You're a fully fledged, platinum-plated terminally-fixated Computer Wally …

But to go back to the games themselves for a moment.

It's surely rather odd that, of the huge number available, so few should relate in any way to the everyday experience of most Wallies. For instance: there are games enabling you to play the role of warlord in a mediaeval Japanese village; there are games in which you battle your way through phantasmagoric mazes, fending off fire-breathing dragons and evil goblins and warlocks. Yet nowhere will you find a game based around the kind of humdrum problems a Computer Wally confronts in his normal daily life – or used to, back in the days when he still had one. The ticklish problem you faced, for example, when you popped round for a housewarming party at your mate Wally's on this vast new Heron Homes estate three miles outside of town, and you clambered into the motor four hours later and it was pitch dark and you couldn't find your way back onto the main road because not only were you stoned out of your brain, but while you'd been busy Getting It Down You, some other Wally had been out and about swapping all the street names round … Or the time you ran out of petrol in the middle of Windsor Safari Park and you made the wife and Little Wally get out and push, and their legs gave out three hundreds yards from the perimeter fence, and all the time there was this dirty great lion sitting on your bonnet until one of the rangers took a pot shot at it with a tranquillizer dart, only he missed and hit Mrs Wally in the bum instead …

Enough raw material there for a couple of really magic

computer games, you would have thought. But no. Perhaps until the games people fill this gap in the market, the best solution is for Wallies everywhere to get together and write a few programs of their own, possibly along the following lines:

Spaceshopper

Saturday morning at the Interplanetary hypermarket. Thrills and spills galore as you steer a trolley with three Wallies in it through milling hordes of humanoids doing the weekend shop. You will be enchanted by the smooth Pixel movement of multi-coloured tubs of pot noodles and bumper bog-roll packs as they cascade realistically to the floor all around you.

Scoring
10 points for every pyramid of baked beans tins you plough into.
50 points for sticking one on the manager.
100 points for paying by cheque at a cash-only till.

Yellow Peril
Bank Holiday time on the planet Wally – and it's your mission to transport the wife and kids to a specially designated Wally picnic site by the side of the roaring six-lane Zong-to-Alphamagnon freeway. The trouble is, Mrs Wally's doing the map-reading! Watch out for the fun as she guides you the wrong way round the interstellar one-way system and you're attacked by marauding intergalactic traffic wardens armed with plasma bolts and delayed-action exploding parking tickets.

Computerbore
The ultimate game of skill and tedium for the real computer wizard. See if you can wipe out an entire army of earthlings one by one, by sending them to sleep with a lethal burst of computer jargon. But mind you don't succumb to brain death yourself!

SOME ABSOLUTELY SUPERWALLY PARTIES

The Twenty-First

Something rather magical happens between two and three in the morning at every twenty-first party that there has ever been. Everybody turns into a Wally for the night.

No one is quite sure how or why this phenomenon takes place. Like the irresistible urge to do a Jimmy Durante imitation which overcomes you whenever there's a plastic cup in your hand, it's part of the wonderful natural world of the Wally that scientists have never been able to explain.

So before you go to a twenty-first, it's wise to have some idea what to expect and to prepare accordingly. Usually the scene is something like this:

a) First of all, there's the Wally in the corner, telling very old, very boring Bernard Manning jokes to a sprawling group of

b) Completely paralytic Wallies who lost consciousness soon after the party had started because they'd already spent the first part of the evening Getting One Down them at the Moon and Parrot, because they needed a few drinks before they could face the idea of going to the party of

c) The Wally whose twenty-first it is, and who's standing in the middle of the floor, trying to look as if he's having a wild time, pretending to be drunk and shouting, 'Come on, everybody, let's get on down and dance!' when actually the only two other people on the dance floor are

d) The Wally and Wallette who arrived groping one another, spent the evening in the corner groping one another, and have just decided to go off and grope each other in the upstairs bedroom, unaware that it's already occupied by

e) The Wally who's just met a Wallette on top of a pile of

overcoats on the bed and is trying to get his leg over, while she's saying she's not like that, not here, we've only just met, it's the wrong time of the month, there's somebody's crash helmet sticking into me and anyway I feel really bad about

f) The Wallette who's sitting at the bottom of the stairs crying drunkenly to herself because no one wants to dance with her and her friend's found a feller and is Getting A Bit upstairs and everyone's looking at her and she hates her new job and she knew she shouldn't have come this evening with this bloody great spot which came up this afternoon and her parents keep dropping hints and saying why hasn't she got a boyfriend like all the other girls and she thinks she really might kill herself which would bloody well show them and she's been on the pill for over six months now without even a chance to see if it works or not and tonight the only boy she got to talk to was

g) The Wally who went to the kitchen to get her a drink two and a half hours ago and who never made it because he threw up all over

h) The Wally who was sitting in the kitchen trying to look above it all and thinking how he's going to describe all this in his novel which he hasn't actually started yet but when he does they'll all realise what he was going through when he was interrupted by people being sick on him, not to mention

i) The hairy Wally who has been wandering around with a disgusting looking dog-end in his hand saying to everybody who'll listen, 'Take a hit of this, man, it's absolutely fucking amaaaaaazing stuff, man' until he makes the mistake of saying it to

j) The Wally from next door who's just walked in wearing pyjamas and said that personally he likes to hear kids having a good time but it really is a bit loud, and it is four in the morning, and his wife has a nervous complaint, and the dog's eating the curtains and, fair's fair, lads, some of us have to get up in the morning to do a day's work, you know, so stop this Wallying about NOW.

The Office Leaving Party

No one except a complete Wally could enjoy these occasions – and of course, they offer unlimited opportunities for Wally behaviour.

Ten minutes after the party has started, the resident Office Wally has already tried to open a wine box with a corkscrew, completely flooding the huge bowl of chewy peanuts which is the only food on offer at the party. He has then proceeded to weave his way among the guests with a flagon of Black Label, spilling most of it on the floor and down people's clothes as he goes. And he's told the Personnel Officer that he's always fancied her, even though she's an older woman of course. She in turn has asked him whether he has ever met her husband who's a strong-arm man with a debt-collection agency, and has made a mental note to put a big, red 'WALLY' sticker on his confidential folder first thing the next morning.

Thirty minutes after the party has started, the Wally has belched his way through the boss's speech, and after the presentation to the person who's leaving, he now stands on a table and makes a highly embarrassing impromptu speech in which he announces that the lads have clubbed together for an extra special present, which turns out to be either *The Sex Maniac's Diary* or *How To Be a Wally*, or, if the person is female and leaving to get married, a maternity gown.

An hour and a half after the party has started, everyone has gone home except him and a clutch of other Office Wallies, who now decide to go out, get totally pissed, and then get a bloody great vindaloo down them at the Jewel in the Crown Tandoori House.

The Porn Video Party

All that's needed for a Porn Video Party is a dozen cans of Black Label, a video, a few like-minded Wallies and copies of *I'm Not Feeling Myself Tonight, Wham Bam Thank You Ma'am!, The Devil in Miss Jones, Emmanuelle Meets Lassie, The Confessions of a Swedish Virgin Nymphomaniac*, and *Some Came Running*. (Cue for 'Who got hold of this load of old rubbish?' 'Sorry, Wall. Must have got it confused with Paul Raymond's sizzling sextravaganza *Can I Come Again, Please?*')

When, at one in the morning, everyone at the party is either asleep or bored senseless by the spectacle of heaving, spotty Scandinavians Getting a Bit on the screen, one Wally suggests ringing up a few Wallettes and inviting them round for some raunchy late-night fun. They talk about this for an hour, then decide it's a bit too late to ring anyone so they all go home.

The Stag Party

Here is the Wally social occasion par excellence – and yet so many Wallies make the mistake of thinking that all you need for a night to remember is a few of the lads, a table for ten at the local restaurant and a Wallette stripogram artiste.

It's not like that at all. It's impossible to achieve a truly Wally occasion without some careful planning. For the perfect Wally stag night, some – if not all – of the following procedures should be adopted:

1) Arrive at the restaurant singing, 'Here we are, Here we are, Here we are', and do the conga to your table. At least two members of your party should already have taken their shirts off and should be waving them over their heads like lassoos.

2) If you've booked a table for ten, there should be at least twelve of you. The two spare Wallies should sit in the middle of the table, on other Wallies' laps or at other guests' tables until someone has somehow managed to fit the extra chairs in.

3) Order ten litres of red and white house wine.

4) Throw buns at the other tables. As a couple nearby hurriedly prepare to leave, burst into song with 'One None, One None, One None.'

5) Take as long as possible to order the meal and kick up a fuss if there are no Whopperburgers on the menu. As the waitress serves it up, make leering gestures to the other Wallies behind her back and gasp randily whenever she leans over the table.

6) If there's live music, request 'Stairway to Heaven'. When they say they don't play it, insist that Wally, who's a really brilliant guitarist, is allowed to get on stage to do a couple of numbers. Throw more buns when they refuse.

7) Sing the pornographic versions of *Alouette, Ilkley Moor* and *The Twelve Days of Christmas*, insisting that everyone else in the restaurant joins in.

8) Table-hop and, putting on a serious 'I'm not really pissed' face, ask all the women, particularly the ones that are obviously married, if they fancy you. In the event of other Wallies beating you to it, stand behind them, singing 'Wally's Got a Big One, Wally's Got a Big One' as they try and chat the women up.

9) Do the conga around the restaurant, dragging other guests up from their tables to join the chain. If possible, lead them into the kitchen and emerge all holding your noses.

10) Grab the microphone from the band and make loud farting noises into it.

11) Stand on the table and moon at other guests.

12) Dance with each other between the tables, trip and collapse, giggling, in a pile of chairs, cutlery and broken plates.

13) Throw some wine glasses at the wall. If anyone objects, say you thought it was the custom in

Greek/Russian/French/Indian/English restaurants.
14) At least one Wally should then cut himself badly on the broken glass and be whisked off to hospital in an ambulance, having bled copiously over everyone.
15) Argue for half an hour over the bill.
16) Leave a 15p tip.
17) Leave the restaurant, weaving between the tables, singing 'Cheerio, Cheerio, Cheerio'.
18) Be violently sick on the steps on your way out.

THE WALLY ENTERTAINER

If there's one thing that marks you out straight away as a truly Advanced Wally, it's your burning desire to get up on your hind legs at the office party, pub, social club or annual Club Wally Talent Contest and make a prize tit of yourself in front of a crowd of other Wallies.

There are various ways in which you can do this: you can show them how you can open a beer bottle with your teeth; you can demonstrate how it's possible to shatter the bottom off a beer bottle by bringing your hand down sharply on the top; you can wow them with the old Clint Eastwood trick of striking a match on your zipper ... But experience shows that there's nothing tickles an audience of Wallies quite as much as when you treat them to your impressions of a few boring old Superwally Celebrities. Try it: they'll split their sides. Alternatively they could just split to the bar. Or pelt you with peanuts and beer cans. Still, as they say, that's showbiz.

A word or two first about technique. The success of any comedy act depends greatly on *timing*, but there's no need to make a fetish of it. As far as a brief comic turn in the saloon bar of the Moon and Parrot goes, any time after six will do. In fact, you could probably give a one-man rendering of the death of Little Nell and there still wouldn't be a dry seat in the house.

Bruce Forsyth

Always a favourite with the punters.

1) Lift right leg, holding it bent at knee. Place knuckles of right hand against forehead:

2) Arrange features in grinning rictus, jutting chin forward as if trying to swallow tip of nose with lower lip:

3) Mince forward to footlights, jerking head back and forth like a turkey. Pause to acknowledge screams of mirth, shouts of GERROFF, WHADDA LOADA RUBBISH etc.

4) Knock them dead with a typical bellybusting Brucie catchphrase, e.g.:

GOOD GAME GOOD GAME

DIDN'T THEY DO WELL *or*

NICE TER SEE YER TER SEE YER …

5) Fling arms forward and *up*:

… NIIIII-CE!

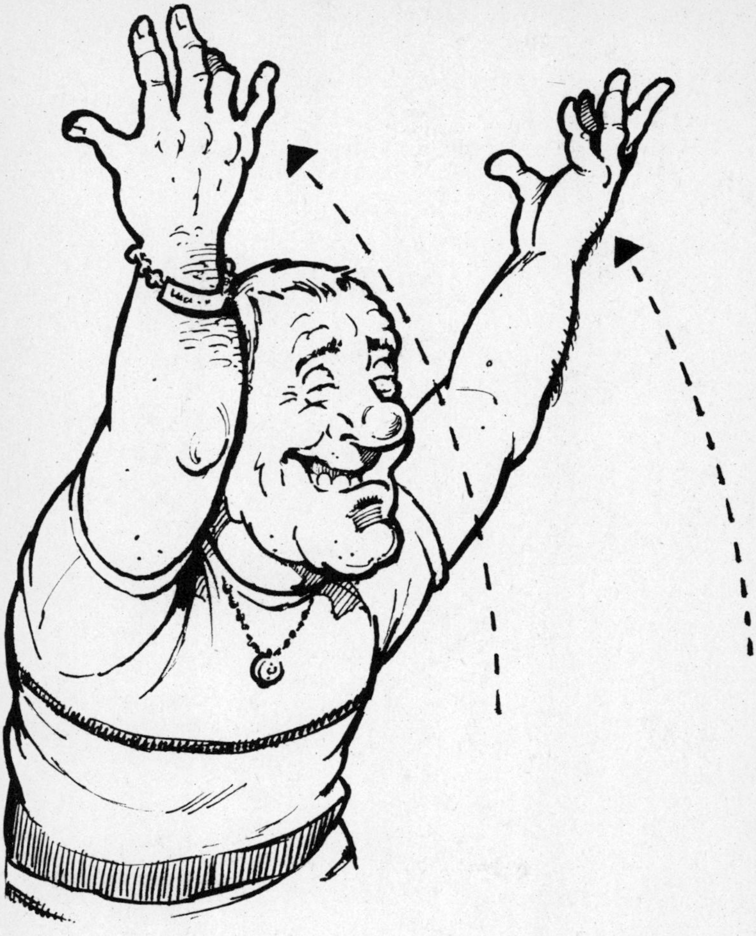

So far so good. Your audience is really falling about at this mesmeric display of top-flight impressionistic skill. You may even find that there's a bit of a hiatus here while the smelling salts are passed around and the stretcher cases removed. So before the rest of the audience have a chance to hotfoot it to the Gents or nearest exit, whip out the old beret and belted mackintosh and hit them with another surefire crowd-pleaser, viz. your patent …

Frank Spenser impression

Another guaranteed winner – and so easy too, given your natural affinity with the role.

1) Pull down beret well over ears.
2) Suck in cheeks; purse lips into pouting 'O' shape. Adopt startled, vaguely indignant expression.

3) Puff out chest; plant right hand on hip; swivel head around gormlessly.
4) Bring the house down with:
MMMM … NICE
OOOOOH … BETTEEEEEE
or
DA DONKEE'S DONE A LIDDEL WHOOPSIE IN DA CORRIDOR

By now there should be total pandemonium out there. They're just wetting themselves. But the fun isn't over yet – not by a long way. There's still Tommy Cooper, Ken Dodd, Larry Grayson and the entire cast of Hi-De-Hi to come, not to mention your grand finale: the bit you copied off Mike Yarwood, where you stuff a ping pong ball in cheek, clamber on top of a bar stool and do an impression of Max Bygraves doing an impression of Michael Foot doing an impression of a dead ostrich singing *You Are My Sunshine* while drinking from a can of Red Stripe ...

Unfortunately what usually happens at this point is that either the Wallies at the back start a slow-handclap, or else the mike is suddenly snatched out of your hand and you find yourself being hustled off stage to make way for some amateur topless go-go dancer, budding Paul Daniels or a blowsy half-sozzled middle-aged Wallette who insists on favouring the assembled company with a selection from *South Pacific*. And the curious thing is, *they* always get a standing ovation. Still, it just highlights one of the problems you face when you perform for Wallies: they just don't know sheer class when it's handed to them on a plate.

THE WALLY COUNTRY CODE

Most people think of the average Wally as a confirmed city-dweller: the type who'd no more dream of escaping to the country in search of pastoral peace and mystic one-ness with Nature than he would of joining MENSA, becoming a Community Service Volunteer, or taking out life-membership of the National Trust. And for ninety-nine per cent of the year, that's probably the case.

And yet from time to time there comes a moment in every Wally's life when he begins to tire of the choking traffic fumes and all the din and confusion of modern city life; when the pleasure of kicking an empty Macdonald's carton up and down a shopping precinct, endlessly doing Kerb Endo's on Little Wally's BMX bike, or gobbing out of car windows at passing pedestrians begins to pall. When, frankly, urban life, with all the splendid opportunities it affords for being a complete and utter Wally, is about as appealing as a three-day-old reheated Chinese Take Away.

At such moments, even the most dedicated Wally feels a vague hankering for something completely different. He yearns for the green fields, the clear blue skies, the wide open spaces. He longs to hear the birds singing in the treetops, the soft, soothing rustle of a gentle summer breeze and the refreshing babble of a nearby brook …

And so, once or twice a year, usually around Bank Holiday time, he loads up the motor with a primus stove, insulated plastic picnic box, twelve cans of Black Label and a giant ghetto blaster and, accompanied by thousands of other Wallies all of whom have experienced exactly the same lemming-like urge, he bids farewell to the city and heads off to the country to lay waste to that instead.

Top Ten Wally Ways to Commune with Nature

Given the appalling lack of really gross Wally pubs in rural areas and the fact that the slightest error in map-reading is liable to land you in the middle of nowhere, miles from the nearest Kentucky and with not a Mecca Entertainments Complex in sight, you might think that opportunities for being a Wally in the countryside are pretty few and far between. Not so. The openings are there *if* you're prepared to look for them. Here are a few suggestion to start you off:

1) Dig up an ancient Druid burial mound on the off-chance of finding a Cadbury-Schweppes Golden Egg at the bottom of it.

2) Attempt to establish an instant rapport with every farm animal in sight by blowing up its nose the Woodhouse way.

3) Swarm into a remote country pub with a crowd of other Wallies and loon around in the snug, doing Walter Gabriel impressions, slopping beer all over the locals and blowing up their nose the Woodhouse way.

4) Select a field criss-crossed with high-voltage electricity cables and steer your radio-controlled Mini Piper Cherokee smack into them.

5) Pick off anything that moves with an air rifle.

6) Get pissed and sit down in a cowpat.

7) Plunder the hedgerows, uprooting wild flowers and sprigs of cow parsley to stick on the front of your motor.

8) Check whether those hours of obedience-training in the park have paid off by letting the Alsatian loose in a field of sheep and ordering it to SIIIIII-*T*.

9) Using a picnic tablecloth, perform a mock-bullfight with the cow in the nextdoor field, then …

10) Discover it's not a cow after all.

WALLY CULTURE

If ever there was proof that the influence of Superwallies in high places is a power for good in this great country of ours, it's the truly heartening rise of Wally Culture.

FACT

We're now exporting more boring old totally non-Wally works of art to gullible American museums than ever before, so that there's more room in our stately homes for frisbee parks, funfairs and dolphinariums.

FACT

The government is very sensibly cutting grants to time-wasting and noisy so-called fringe theatre companies, so that instead of staging hysterical playlets about Soweto, pubs can once more use their upstairs rooms for profitable and worthwhile purposes: snooker, aerobics classes, mud-wrestling and so on.

FACT

The only plays running in the West End are now exclusively written by, acted by, and performed for Wallies. Classics like *No Sex Please, We're Wallies, The Real Wally* and *Wally Pulls it Off* are playing to packed houses of delighted Wallies, as well as coachloads of bewildered foreigners anxious to discover why London is now renowned as the home of Wally theatre.

So pervasive is the influence of Wally Culture that many of our top playwrights are actually revising earlier work in order to keep pace with the times. Possibly the most successful revison was by Harold Pinter, who chucked out all his pre-Wally rubbish and replaced it with such classics as *Wally Comes Home*:

ACT I, SCENE 1

A Wally: It's a bloody choker, it is.

Another Wally: Right.

They stare at the audience for several minutes.

A Wally: A bloody choker.

Another Wally: This is it.

They stare at the audience for several minutes.

Another Wally: When would that be then?

A Wally: Eh?

Another Wally: I said when would that be?

They stare at the audience for several minutes.

A Wally: What were you talking about.

Another Wally: When?

A Wally: Just then. You said 'When would that be then?' I heard it quite distinctly. I've got a good memory for that sort of thing. 'When would that be?' you said. I didn't understand. You lost me.

Another Wally: Oh. I meant, 'When did you choke her?'

A Wally: When did I choke who?

Another Wally: Her, you Wally. I heard you say it. You said you'd bloody choke her. It sounded interesting. Different. Not the sort of thing you hear every day. People don't talk about choking each other every day. They talk about being cheesed off about things. Browned off. The wife doesn't understand me. Gets on my wick. Gets my dander up. That sort of thing. But not 'I'm going to bloody choke her'. Not often anyway.

<u>A Wally</u>: No, I suppose not. I don't know. I'm confused now. I wasn't. Confused, that is. But I am now. I never knew I had a wife.

<u>They both stare at the audience for several minutes</u>.

<u>End of Act I</u>

Wally Shakespeare

It's an enterprise that has grabbed the imagination of Wally educationalists from Milton Keynes to Leighton Buzzard: the complete rewriting of the works of Shakespeare, so that, instead of being in unintelligible and totally old-fashioned English which, let's face it, no one speaks these days, the Bard's great masterpieces will be translated into so-called 'Wallyspeak' and so be made accessible to Wallies everywhere.

The person behind the idea is none other than Dr Dick Wally, the Leicester University academic whose Wally version of Hamlet's 'To be or not to be/That is the question' speech ('To go for the big one or not to go for the big one/At the end of the day that's basically what it's all about') was widely praised.

Here then are two versions of Act IV Scene 7 of *Henry V* – the boring, old original version and the exciting new, Dick Wally version:

WILLIAM SHAKESPEARE

K. Hen: I was not angry since I came to France
Until this instant. Take a trumpet, herald;
Ride thou unto the horseman on yon hill;
If they will fight with us, bid them come down,
Or void the field; they do offend our sight.....

WALLY SHAKESPEARE

K. Hen: I kid you not, I'm as sick as a bloody parrot. In my book, the Frogs are way out of order on this one. It's on yer bike time - bloody shit or get off the pot, if you'll pardon my French. And we won't be pardoning theirs - ber-boom!

Exeter: Here comes the herald of the French, my liege.

Gloucester: His eyes are humbler than they us'd to be.

K. Hen: How now! What means this, herald? know'st thou not
That I have fin'd these bones of mine for ransom?
Com'st thou again for ransom?

Exeter: Say no more, Hen. Talk of the devil - here he comes now.

Gloucester: No way is that one happy Frenchman.

K. Hen: Hop off, you Frogs.

Sounds Wally

These days, an awful lot of Wallies still seem to think that when it comes to music, you can't beat a blast of Frankie Goes to Hollywood, Kajagoogoo, or, if you're into Heavy Metal, the latest single from Motorhead – which is fine if you've got Heinz Vegetable Salad where your brains used to be and you happen to thrill to the sound of a million crashing dustbin lids and pneumatic road drills (and of course, you do).

But ever since the LSO made their successful bid for Wally credibility by throwing together a hotch-potch of classical numbers, slapping on a disco beat and releasing it as a chart-topping 45, a lot of today's more advanced and sophisticated Wallies have realized that to get ahead of the pack, sound-wise, you have to go one better: you have to get switched on to the Classics too.

What – Beethoven? Tchaikovsky? Stuff like that? Leave it out ...

Okay. Admittedly you can't always pogo or break-dance to them, but some of those evergreen classical sounds are terrific for headbanging, and anyway, even if you never actually play them, a couple of classical albums can look pretty impressive peeking out from among the Duran Duran singles and Mum's TV theme-tune compilations.

But supposing you're pig-ignorant about classical music? Supposing you thought that Handel's Largo came in cans? Where do you start?

No problem.

Because nowadays all an Advanced Wally has to do to get himself a reputation for genuine musical taste and discernment is to cut along to the local Boots or John Menzies and check out

THE WALLYDISC CLASSICS FOR PLEASURE COLLECTION

Now, a lot of the sleeve-notes on the more upmarket classical labels can be a bit unhelpful, not to say intimidating for the novice. For instance, does any Wally seriously want to know that Bach wrote his famous Air on a

Slim Panatella in the year sixteen-whatever-it-was in response to a commission from the Kapellmeister of the Leipzig-a-Go-Go Discorama? Or that Mozart's Concerto for Colonel Bogey Car Horn was first performed by Wolfgang and the lads while they were Getting One Down them in the back of a coach in a lay-by on the Salzburg by-pass?

No. What you're interested in is the music: what to play, when to play it, and how to pass the time while you're pretending to listen to it. So with this in mind, Wallydisc have prepared their own Classical Hit Parade, plus a few helpful tips designed to maximise your listening pleasure.

Top Ten Wallydisc Classical Pops of All Time

1) *Tchaikovsky: the Dance of the Sugar-Plum Fairy*
Light, fluffy and tinkling. Play it as you prance round the lounge in your new Adidas trainers.
2) *Ravel's Bolero*
Perfect Saturday night leg-over music. Or of course you can ice-skate to it …
3) *Richard Strauss: Thus Spake Zarathustra*
That's the 2001 theme to you. Beat time with a rolled copy of *Smash Hits* or scrape away at an imaginary violin.
4) *Rachmaninov: Rhapsody on a Theme of Paganini*
Watch out for the slushy bit that goes da da-da-da-da *dum dum* … One for the Mums and Dads.
5) *Mendelssohn: Fingal's Cave*
Very boring. Nothing much you can do with this except sit down and listen to it.
6) *Tchaikovsky: Swan Lake*
To remind you of the time you nearly bagged one with Little Wally's air rifle.
7) *Rimsky-Korsakov; the Flight of the Bumble Bee*
To remind you of the time you nearly bagged Little Wally with Little Wally's air rifle.
8) *Chopin: Preludes*
Moody and soulful. Have a good blub to it after watching the lads get hammered Five Nothing in the EUFA Cup qualifier.

9) *Tchaikovsky: 1812 Overture*
World War Three erupts in your own living room. Just the job for Lads' Night, Cup Final Night, or breaking the furniture at parties.

10) *Beethoven's Choral Symphony*
Heavy but fun. Play it full-volume on the car stereo. It'll give a whole new meaning to the Sound of Happy Motoring.

The Wally Walkman

POLITICS: THE ART OF THE SUPERWALLY

In no sphere of modern life is the rise and rise of the Superwally more evident and noticeable than the world of politics.

The time when politicians merely needed to be neatly dressed, well connected and at least semi-literate is truly dead and gone. Now that Wallies form such an important and growing part not only of the electorate itself but also of the media, the only way to the top of the greasy pole is for every politician to try and prove to the world that he is a bigger Wally or Wallette than his or her opponent.

Not surprisingly, this trend started in America. The experts are divided as to who precisely was the first leading American politican to show that, if you can prove to the nation that you are unquestionably a Superwally, then power and success will soon be within your grasp. Some say it was Lyndon Johnson picking his beagle up by the ears for the television cameras; others that it was Gerald Ford falling down the steps of Airforce One. Then there was George McGovern crying like a Wally, Edward Kennedy driving like a Wally, and Jimmy Carter collapsing in the middle of a fun run in a spectacularly Wally way – all culminating in the moment when the man who has truly given the term 'Superwally' international significance ambled photogenically into the White House four years ago.

Not that we in Britain have lagged behind. No one could argue that the country that has produced men of the stature of George Brown, Sir Alec Douglas-Home, Edward Heath and Cyril Smith has failed to keep pace with the world development of Superwallies in politics over the last twenty years.

These days, politicians everywhere are recognizing that the so-called Wally Factor is an important part of their public image and are now working on new techniques to show the voters what complete and utter Wallies they all are.

Among the more successful methods are:

The Skinner Skinhead
Now very popular among backbench MPs who like to see their names in the papers, this method involves jumping up and down in the House of Commons, shouting, swearing, going red in the face and calling everyone a bloody liar until eventually the Speaker shows you the red card. Dennis Skinner, the original Skinhead, is now regarded as the Wally To Watch on the Labour backbenches.

The Williams Wobble
A simple device for winning affection and easy laughs, the Williams Wobble involves missing every important train by at least five minutes and always arriving late and breathless for interviews. Shirley Williams, who created this technique, applied it to perfection when she managed to arrive too late to catch a launch which was to carry the SDP leaders down the Thames as part of a campaign to establish them as the party of efficiency and unity.

The Parkinson Peccadillo
A tricky manoeuvre for all but the most adept Wallies, the Parkinson Peccadillo involves looking like Mr Clean, being widely tipped as a future prime minister, getting caught with your trousers down and then being brought back to public life as the saviour of the government after a *Daily Mail* campaign. After all, any old Wally can make a mistake, can't he?

The Hailsham Dotty Old Peer Routine
Perfected over many years as a Superwally, the Hailsham Dotty Old Peer Routine involves behaving like an ageing Billy Bunter on speed, making fatuous remarks about anything that takes your fancy, losing your temper for absolutely no reason and wearing silly hats when there are cameras about.

The Howe Amiable Bungle
Invented by the well-known Conservative foreign secretary, this technique involves shuffling around looking embarrassed, talking in a funereal monotone normally reserved for Speak-Your-Weight machines, blinking a lot when interviewed and losing your trousers on a train carrying every political journalist in the country.

TRUE CONFESSIONS

No Superwally likes to feel totally uninformed about what's going on in the world around him. While the mere Wally may be proud of his ignorance and work daily to increase it, the Superwally will tirelessly keep up with the news that matters – politics, the economy, the Embassy World Snooker Championships, and how busty Page Three Girl Katrina has big plans to be an actress (and we're sure you'll agree she's got great prospects before her!)

So he reads the soaraway *Sun*.

The most memorable item for *Sun* Superwallies in recent times (apart from 'RANDY ANDY'S HANKY SPANKY!', 'BASTARD! *Sun* readers blast "Adolf" Scargill', and "EMERY WAS FLOP IN BED", says Dick's frilly-knicker sex siren') was the news that Wallies all over the country were to be given the chance to confess their crimes to their favourite newspaper. But although several major unsolved cases were cleared up this way, there were several Wally confessions that were considered too shocking, even for *Sun* readers …

'I slept with our sixteen-year-old babysitter'

'I just can't think what came over me. I'm a happily married man with a gorgeous wife, two lovely kids and a nice home, but I once did something that has kept me awake at nights just thinking about it.

'It was when the kids were quite young. The wife and I went out to a party and I suppose the truth is that I'd had one or two too many. I offered to take our young babysitter, an attractive, curvaceous sixteen-year-old called Barbara back to her home. Her parents were away and she asked me if I'd like to come in for a quick cup of tea. Well, one thing led to another and, by the end of the first cup, I was pretty sure that this young girl was eager for a sizzling sex session with me on the settee. Unfortunately I was so pissed that, before I could even suggest a quick one, I passed out on the floor. My wife has always been suspicious about why I came back so late that night, but I've never been able to tell her the full story.

'Now I can't sleep at night for thinking that Busty Barbara, the sexy schoolgirl siren of the baby-sitting circle, could have been mine for the night. But just telling the soaraway *Sun* makes me feel better already!'

Terry, Luton

'It was just a lark for us – but seventeen cars, a couple of innocent bystanders and a mongrel puppy paid a terrible price.'

'I was out with a couple of the lads, and we thought it would be a bit of a giggle if we turned round some traffic diversion signs so that a few motors would be sent round the one-way system in our town the wrong way. Well, it worked a treat – not even the ambulances could get through the debris. Then we smashed a few windows, nutted someone who was winding us up by looking at us, nutted someone else who was winding us up by refusing to look at us, tipped up a milk float and attached a banger to a dog's tail to see what would happen. Then we booked a punter for a flagrant double yellow line traffic violation and went back to the station.

'The sarge said it was a good day's work, but I've always had a nagging feeling that what we did wasn't quite right.'

PC Trevor, Derby

'I'm a spoilt Wally Hooray and I love every minute of it'

'I've always felt rather awful about spending public money wining and dining a string of randy models, prancing about naked with Vicki Hodge on the sun-drenched island of Mustique, getting spanked by topless waitresses in suspender belts, asking Selina Scott if she'd like to come round the back of the studio in the middle of an interview, and, the only time I was asked to do anything remotely serious, spraying journalists with white paint and then braying with laughter. I read the *Sun* every day and love all the bits I can understand. My head hurts now so I'd better stop.'

Darren, Buckingham Palace, London

'I Got One Down me what I shouldn't of'

'I told my mate I got 795 on the Asteroids at the Moon and Parrot when I'd really only got 10. He only managed to get 5 so he had to buy me a pint.'

Pete, Newcastle

'Could my boyish prank have changed the course of modern history?'

'I'm in my fifties now, but I feel very bad about something that happened when I was a 'slip of a lad' back in 1963. I was on holiday in America staying with these friends in Texas. The son of the family was called Mitch, and we lads used to go to nearby Dallas with a rifle – there was an old warehouse there and we used to shoot beer cans off a roof over the other side of the road. One fateful day, there were a lot of people milling about on the street below. We'd had a bit to drink, and when it came to my shot, I tripped and shot down into the street instead of across it. I may be wrong, but I thought I saw someone in an open-top limousine fall down as he was waving to a friend. I hope and pray I'm wrong, but I've always been haunted by the thought that our silly prank may have had serious consequences.'

Ginger, Tonbridge Wells

THE INNER WALLY

Wallies have psychological crises in their lives just like anyone else – and it's no use their family and friends saying, 'Wally's just being a bigger Wally than he normally is' and thinking that the problem will go away. Someone suffering in this way needs to be nursed through the dark clouds of gloom, depression and self-doubt to the sunny skies beyond, so that they can be the familiar carefree Wally that you knew of old.

Above all, remember that psychological crises can be serious. In some cases, days of introspection, worry and guilt can cause such a radical transformation of character that, by the end of it all, the sufferer is a Wally in name only.

Following recent violent incidents caused by Spurs and Chelsea Wallies in Europe, the government commissioned a report by a team of psychologists, whose brief was to study in detail the Wally lifestyle and Wally habits and behaviour. At the time many people were puzzled by the move: after all, why should a series of perfectly healthy Wally incidents, only marred by a typically cynical over-reaction by foreign policemen using incredible violence to break up quite innocent looting parties, be thought to require an investigation into so-called hang-ups and problems? The only explanation was that the growing Wally faction in Whitehall (see *Politics: the Art of the Superwally*) must have been behind it all.

Yet the experts' findings did, after all, have some relevance. They concluded that the average Wally experiences what they call The Five Crises in his life. So here is a brief account of how each of those crises feels to the Wally, with appropriate remedies:

Crisis One: Childhood

At the age of about seven, a conflict within Little Wally's subconscious comes to boiling-point. On one side, he's feeling, 'I don't really *want* to pull down saplings in the park and have swordfights with the other little Wallies like in *Robin of Sherwood.* I'd like to stay at home, read a book, listen to some early Chopin preludes and learn the rudiments of chess.'

Meanwhile, the other side of his subconscious is telling him: 'Leave it out, Wally. If Dad wanted to have a little ponce sitting at home playing with his rudiments, he'd have had a little girl, wouldn't he? So on yer bike, my son, and you're the sheriff.'

Solution: Promise the little brat an A-team sweat shirt if he swears never to look at another book. Then lock up the nancy-boy classical records, with the possible exception of *Hooked on Classics* and *Cats.*

Crisis Two: Adolescence

The Wally has reached a stage in his life when he's beginning to have trouble with girls. The problem is, he likes them. He dreams of having conversations and meaningful relationships with them, and makes secret plans for a long weekend in Paris in the hope of finally meeting the girl of his dreams. He tries hard to join in with the other Wallies and say, 'Gor, catch a load of that' whenever he sees a girl go by in a tight T-shirt, but, in his heart of hearts, he'd like to go up to her and say something sweet and understanding that will show her he's not like all the other boys.

Solution: Find a Wallette who's not likely to fall for all this Mills and Boon slop. Make it worth her while – promise her a Radio One biro or something – and get her to take him round the back of the Moon and Parrot for a quick knee-trembler. When she rejoins the other Wallettes at the bar, she should make loud references to Wee Willie Winkie.

As everyone in the pub rocks with laughter, his attitude towards women will improve immediately.

Crisis Three: Fatherhood

The Wally looks back on his life so far and, for a moment, it seems to him a desolate wasteland of empty beer-cans, smashed supermarket trollies, inflated condoms and cheap motor accessories, all signifying very little. Then he looks at Little Wally as he puts the finishing touches to a spring trap which will catapult the neighbour's ginger cat fifty feet in the air the next time it sets foot in the back yard, and he wonders whether he shouldn't be showing him a better way forward – perhaps the occasional book, a chess set, or a recording of *Chopin's Greatest Hits* on Classics for Pleasure.

Solution: Try it. After killing the neighbour's cat, Little Wally will use the chess pieces for target practice with his air rifle and the record as a frisbee. Face it – being a complete and utter Wally is in the blood and nothing's going to shift it.

Crisis Four: Middle Age

The years are beginning to take their toll on the Wally. He'd prefer to watch *Crossroads* than spend the evening Getting a Few Down him at the Moon and Parrot. And, even when he is out with the lads, he feels a bit queasy after his ninth pint. It doesn't feel right playing football with a beercan in the car park any more and, at the Christmas party, when the Office Wallette suggests their annual visit to the firm's store-room to check stock-levels, his heart sinks and he cries off, claiming that Mrs Wally was suspicious last Christmas when she found wood shavings in his Y-fronts. He watches *The Price is Right* every week, but even that makes him feel a bit tired. Frankly, life's a bit of a choker these days.

Solution: There's basically no solution to the Wally's mid-life crisis, beyond accepting the fact that only people like Patrick Moore and Ted Rogers can manage to be complete and utter Wallies all their lives – and even that took them years of practice.

Crisis Five: Old Age

What good is a Wally who can hardly lift a can of Black Label, let alone Get It Down him? Who's such a menace on the roads that no one lets him near his old Escort, which is gathering dust in the garage? Who gets jostled down at the Moon and Parrot by a new generation of Wallies not interested in his Wally tales of yore: the day we got to the Membury service station in 22½ minutes flat; the day we gave the Wallette behind the bar a vibrator and she thought it was for curling her hair; the day we saw the late, great Dickie Davies at the local darts championship and I asked him ... Leave it out, Grandad, Wally tales of yawn, more like, eh lads?

Solution: Apart from filling up his time with totally useless activities (See *Occupational Therapy for the Elderly Wally*), there's sadly not much that can be done for this decrepit old Wally as he shuffles his way towards the front of the queue for the Great Shopping Precinct in the sky.

OCCUPATIONAL THERAPY FOR THE ELDERLY WALLY

Just because the Elderly Wally doesn't rush about in the way he used to, there's no reason to think that he can't pursue Wally activities in his own quiet, utterly senile way. Try some of these occupational exercises to keep him more or less alert and fill in those long, empty hours between *Crossroads* episodes:

1) Attach a Woolworth's Old Folks' Home Head-Banger to the back of his armchair. Whenever an old Status Quo number comes up on one of Golden Oldies slots on the radio, he can pull it round in front of him and hammer his grizzled old head against the cushioned board just like when he was a lad.
2) Give him some motor accessories that you've picked up cheap from a bric-a-brac shop and get him to fix them on his wheelchair. It'll take him days to fit the Go-Faster stripes, Radio 2 sun vizor, nodding dog, roll bar and Colonel Bogey hooter. Once he's done it, tell him not to be such a silly old fool and that he'd better dismantle it all before he gets too excited.
3) Get him to crochet a cover for next door's Cortina. When he's finished that, tell him that the caravan could do with one too.
4) Buy him five hundred large boxes of matches and tell him to get on with building a matchstick model of Blackpool pier, the Hammersmith Palais, the Kop or the Taj Mahal. (No, not the new Indian restaurant on the High Street, you silly old goat, the famous wonder of the world.)
5) Encourage him to develop an intimate daily relationship with the television newsreaders. Hardly a

day will go by without the old Wally puzzling over such questions as:

- What Jan Leeming's done with her hair tonight
- Whether Alastair Burnett has grown snootier to the other readers since he got his knighthood
- Why Carol Barnes always reaches for a glass of water so eagerly at the end of the news
- Whether it's really water
- If Andrew Gardner is just saying, 'Well done, lass,' to Tina Jenkins when they dim the lights at the end of news, or if he's asking her whether she fancies getting the hell out of this dump, going to a disco in Mayfair, bopping to the wee small hours and then back to his place to go over the main points again?

WHAT TO DO WITH A DEAD WALLY'S ASHES

No Wally would like to think that he'll be completely forgotten after he's Gone for the Big One for positively the last time. Not for him a dignified burial in the peaceful country churchyard where the bones of his ancestors have lain for generations. Even in death, he wants to be where the action is.

So as well as clubbing together to buy some fitting memorial to him – a park bench for other Wallies to tip up and scratch their names on, say, or a commemorative trough in the Gents at Stamford Bridge – his grieving relatives should make sure that Wally's mortal remains are preserved in the quiet, tasteful way he would have liked.

Choosing a suitable final resting place for your Dear Departed is bound to be a painful and harrowing task, but here are a few suggestions:

- In an engraved tankard behind the bar at the Moon and Parrot
- On the starting grid at Brands Hatch
- In his best mate Wally's petrol tank ('Good old Wally – bloody joker to the last')
- In a coffee jar in the lounge

This last idea was in fact popularized by none other than Superwallette Fay Hiller, Dick Emery's frilly-knicker sex siren, who revealed that she had stolen some of the zany comedian's mortal remains after the cremation and now keeps them in a love-shrine in her sitting room. (Most Wally families should probably avoid this, for fear of serving up cups of Wally in mistake for Maxwell House at the monthly Ann Summers Sex Accessory coffee morning.)

Top Ten Wally ways of trying to raise money for a Kidney Machine

1. Sitting on a pavement from the 10th December to the 1st January in a bid to beat the world record for queueing for the January sales.
2. Getting a leg amputated and hopping from Land's End to John O'Groats.
3. Talking for over sixty hours without a break to David Hamilton and suffering permanent brain damage as a result.
4. Getting sponsored for the London Marathon and collapsing after half a mile.
5. Going up to someone and saying, 'I'm collecting money for a kidney machine or something, give us some'.
6. Collecting 100,000 beer tops and then discovering that they should have been milk bottle tops instead.
7. Going on a sponsored pub crawl where the sponsor had to buy all the drinks.
8. Phoning in a pledge of £100 to Terry Wogan's BBC Telethon and then realising that you're meant to *collect* £100, not give it away.
9. Trying to run the full length of the Great North Road attached to a kidney machine.
10. Getting buried fifty feet under the ground for a month by which time everyone has forgotten all about you.

Top Ten Wally Conversational Topics

1. Dick Emery's amazing showgirl love-nest shock secret.
2. Whether Torvil and Dean are just good friends or whether he gives her the occasional Triple Lutz in the dressing room after the show.
3. Which of the Coronation Street cast will be the next to die, get busted, or be caught with his pants down.
4. Our Boys in Blue, God Bless 'Em.
5. This new government bill to stop poofs from molesting innocent police officers who from time to time in the normal exercise of their duties quite understandably wander into notorious Soho gay bars dressed in black leather and hang around waiting for some pervert to sidle up to them and suggest a bit of hanky-panky in the Gents.
6. The latest totally unjustifiable attempt by some limp-wristed bloody Leftie in the Home Office to prevent the National Front from exercising their inalienable democratic right to march down the local High Street, smash up an Asian deli or two and knock a few nignogs' heads together.
7. The latest vicious and totally unjustifiable prison sentences meted out to a few high-spirited British lads who went over to Luxembourg for the Big One and got a bit carried away I grant you.
8. The latest shock-horror rapist scare and what you'd like to do if you ever got your hands on the bastard responsible mind you if you want my opinion any girl who's out on her own at that time of night is bloody well asking for trouble.
9. The case for reviving the good old mediaeval practice of hanging, drawing and quartering then carrying the victim's head through the streets of London on a pole, and how personally you're not a violent man but when you see the kind of crimes people commit nowadays you'd be only too happy to do the job yourself.
10. Who Ernie will get to replace Eric.

Top Ten Wally Bodily Ailments

1 Jogger's Nipple
2 Medallion Rash
3 Saturday Night Fever
4 Docker's Armpit
5 Brewer's Droop
6 Cauliflower Ear
7 Double vision
8 Chronic flatulence
9 Acne
10 Undescended testicles

Top Ten Wallies who Went for The Big One but found themselves in All Sorts Of Trouble when The Chips Were Down

1 The Wally who tried to row the Atlantic in a four-foot boat. (He made it.)
2 The Wally waitress who gave Prince Andrew a spanking. (Her boss grabbed all the publicity.)
3 The Wally on the *Mail On Sunday* who thought that flying a mangy Libyan rabbit back from Tripoli and headlining the story 'HONEYBUN'S HOME' would increase circulation. (It did.)
4 The double-barrelled Wally who set out to walk to the North Pole, then had to be airlifted home a couple of days later suffering from frostbite and a sprained ankle. (He succeeded on his next attempt.)
5 The Wally who jumped off Clifton Suspension Bridge dressed up as Santa Claus with an elastic band round his waist. (He should have done it in the nude.)
6 The Wally Cambridge Cox who thought he was in the high hurdles and steered the boat into Hammersmith Bridge. (He made the whole dull old sporting ritual worth watching for a change.)
7 The Wally Test Match streaker who dashed across the pitch waving his arms and brought all play to a standstill. (He forgot to remove his Y-fronts.)
8 The two Danish Wallies who had a few too many and sawed the arm off the Little Mermaid. (They brought it back the next morning.)
9 The protesting Greenpeace Wallies who shinned up Big Ben and draped a couple of banners over it to draw attention to the government's policy on nuclear waste. (They should have done it just for a lark.)
10 The Wally newspaper editor who sued the BBC's *Week Ending* programme for describing him as a brainless yobbo. (He should have taken it as a compliment.)

Top Ten Wally things to do with a Football Scarf

1 Tie it to the car aerial as you drive off with a load of other Wallies to see the Big One at Stamford Bridge.
2 Chase after other Wallies at a motorway service station, whirling it round your head, making silly whooping noises and pretending it's a lassoo.
3 Stuff it down the front of your trousers and jerk your pelvis lasciviously at female passers-by.
4 Drop your trousers, wrap it round your waist and mince up and down on top of a table like a model in a mini-skirt.
5 Use it as a boxing glove as you hammer the fruit machine in a pathetic attempt to make it cough up some money.
6 Have a tug of war with it over one of the partitions in the Gents.
7 Be sick into it.
8 Get confused in your drunken excitement at the match and throw it on to the pitch thinking it's a toilet roll.
9 Pretend to hang yourself with it after the boys got well and truly stuffed Five Nothing at Stamford Bridge.
10 Succeed.

Top Ten Wally Football Clubs

1. Chelsea
2. Birmingham
3. Millwall
4. Celtic
5. Wolves
6. Grimsby Town
7. Luton
8. Mönchengladbach
9. Manchester City
10. Leyton Orient

Top Ten Wally Newspaper Columns

1 Queen of the Box Nina Myskow's Wally of the Week.
2 Straight Talk by Plain John Smith.
3 Claude Duval, the Punter's Pal.
4 Roderick Mann, the Man the Stars Talk To.
5 Stafford Hildren, The Man Inside your Telly.
6 Godfrey Smith.
7 Me and My Mum.
8 Joe Ashton, the Voice of the People.
9 Dear Unity's Advice Straight From The Heart.
10 Felicity Hawkins' Soap People.

Top Ten Wally Sports

1 Snooker
2 Darts
3 Windsurfing
4 Playing football with a beer can
5 Parascending
6 Motocross
7 Ice-skating
8 Matchplay bowls
10 Rally driving

Top Ten Wally Careers

1. Stripping vicar
2. Policeman
3. Radio One disc jockey
4. Doorstep aluminium double-glazing salesman
5. Professional ballroom-dancer
6. Minister for Drought
7. Motorcycle stunt-rider
8. The SAS
9. Professional lookalike
10. Human cannonball

THE SUPERWALLY CHARTS

Superwally Groups

1 The Barron Knights
2 Status Quo
3 The Bee Gees
4 Bananarama
5 Marillion
6 Instant Sunshine
7 The King's Singers
8 The Nolan Sisters
9 Queen
10 Sky

Superwally Solo Artists

1 Barry Manilow
2 Max Bygraves
3 Shakin' Stevens
4 Julio Iglesias (except when he's singing with Willy Nelson)
5 Richard Clayderman
6 Rod Stewart
7 Demis Roussos
8 Any chat show host who tries to sing (particularly Des O'Connor and Bob Monkhouse)
9 Lena Zavaroni
10 Neil

Top Ten Wally Articles of Faith

1 The two Wallies in *The Professionals* do all their own stunts.
2 *The Thornbirds* was filmed on location in the Australian outback.
3 Ninety per cent of road accidents are caused by people driving too slowly.
4 England would have the best football team in the world if they just had a striker of the class of Platini.
5 All Oriental women have crooked vaginas.
6 Mrs Thatcher is an ordinary housewife and mother.
7 Boy George is not just a pretty face.
8 Your No. 1 *Sun* is the only paper that gives you a true picture of what's really going on.
9 Christmas is for the kids.
10 The British Rail 24-Hour Breakfast is *not* so called because it was cooked 24 hours before you get to eat it.

Superwally Comedians

1 Jim Davison
2 Little and Large
3 Marti Caine
4 Bernard Manning
5 Bruce Forsyth
6 Cannon and Ball
7 Terry Scott
8 Max Bygraves
9 Jimmy Tarbuck
10 Tim Brooke-Taylor

Superwally TV Personalities

1 Jeremy Beadle
2 David Vine
3 Leslie Crowther
4 Jonathan King
5 Barry Took
6 Kenny Everett
7 Kenny Lynch
8 Russell Grant
9 Max Bygraves
10 Jimmy Savile

1 Joan Collins
2 Victoria Principal
3 Prince Andrew
4 Elizabeth Taylor
5 David Frost
6 Omar Sharif
7 Ronald Reagan
8 Sylvester Stallone
9 Andrew Lloyd Webber
10 Torvill and Dean
11 Max Bygraves